Craig Ferguson

Biography

A World of Wit

TABLE CONTENTS

Chapter 1: A Seat at the Table

Chapter 2: Frank Sinatra and Elizabeth Taylor

Chapter 3: The Attic

Chapter 4: Astronaut

Chapter 5: Brick House

Chapter 6: The Filth and the Fury

Chapter 7: The Real World

Chapter 8: Love and Sex

Chapter 9: A Clever and Patient Monster

Chapter 10: Tripping

Chapter 11: New York

Chapter 12: Adventures in the Big City

Chapter 13: Setting the Tone

Chapter 14: The Gong Show

Chapter 15: The Rise of Hitler

Chapter 16: On the Train

Chapter 17: Jimmy's Wedding

Chapter 18: The Aspirations of a Phoney Englishman

Chapter 19: The End of Daze

Chapter 20: Rehab

Chapter 21: Reboot

Chapter 22: Buying a Knife

Chapter 23: The Aspirations of a Phoney Frenchman

Chapter 24: The Fat Man, the Gay Man, Vampires, and Marriage

Chapter 25: Success and Failure

Chapter 26: Crash

Chapter 27: Latecomer

Chapter 28: Riding the Pass

Chapter 29: Settling Down

Chapter 30: American on Purpose

Chapter 1: A Seat at the Table

I saw England, France, and the first lady's underwear."

"Shut up," Megan growled. "I wish I had never pointed it out." She was laughing so hard that wine squirted out of her nose, yet it was real. Laura Bush, the friendly Texan wife of George, the forty-third and possibly least popular president in American history, had just entered the room, her smiling husband by her side. They were gently recognizing the adoring Washington toadies who surrounded them, smiling, shaking hands, and kissing cheeks. Mrs. Bush was dressed elegantly in silk, but as she stood with the light behind her, her underpants were visible. Big, comfortable knickers in what appeared to be a floral pattern, known in enlightened circles as passion killers. Ideal for a long night of smiling, nodding, and being a good sport at the annual White House Correspondents' Association Dinner, which pits the press, showbiz, and politics against each other.

I was there as the rude lounge entertainer. Megan, my date, was there because she loves me and wanted to prove it. The chair of the entertainment committee had invited me to be the guest speaker. I wasn't their first pick, but after Steve Carell and Ellen DeGeneres declined, I believe I became more enticing. I was a C-lister, but I was available, willing, and inexpensive.

I understand why Ellen and Steve said no, because this is without a doubt one of the most scary and challenging jobs a comedian can have. There were other reasons why I should have politely declined as well. First and foremost, there was the event's recent history. Stephen Colbert had performed there two years previously and, depending on who you ask, had either died the worst death ever seen by a comedian in the history of comedy and death, or had delivered the most courageous act of political satire this country had ever seen.

In an attempt to avoid a repeat of the issue, the WHCA engaged the antediluvian Canadian impressionist Rich Little, who rose to popularity in the 1970s with his Richard Nixon impersonation, to be the after-dinner speaker the following year. Little had unquestionably flopped (no discussion) in a buttock-clenchingly embarrassing manner; his content was too antique and timid for the ravenous mob.

I should also have said no because it's the granddaddy of all company events: a huge dinner in a hotel ballroom where everyone secretly despises and wishes disaster on everyone else. Although I've lived in Hollywood for fifteen years, this is not normally a conducive environment for comedy.

I should have said no because the hotel's sound system was so bad that no one in the first two rows of tables could comprehend what was being said, Scottish accent or not.

But I didn't refuse. I didn't say no because, given the choice between safety and adventure, I chose the latter. Plus, meeting all these muckety mucks sounded like fun, and as a new American, I felt it would be unpatriotic to turn down the chance to embarrass myself in front of the president, who, after all, had no problem doing so in front of the entire world.

Backstage before the lunch, there had been a small gathering for those who would be sitting on the dais and their partners, however the only spouses at the head table would be the pleasantly arsed Mrs. Bush and Mrs. Cheney, wife of Dirty Dick.

It was a time for everyone to meet and talk before we went out on stage and sat in a line like the image of the Last Supper.

We met Richard Wolfe, the astute MSNBC political commentator and Olbermann henchman, who convinced me after a brief talk that Barack Obama will be the next President of the United States. This still shocks me, because Obama didn't even have the Democratic nomination at the time.

Dick was unexpectedly personable and had a croaky easy laugh, but I had the distinct sensation that I was in the midst of a Bond villain. All he needed was a pussy to stroke, preferably not in front of the grandchildren.

We chatted briefly before the Cheneys went on to the next gladhanders. After they'd left, I told Megan that Dick Cheney had been admiring her breasts.

"Nah," she replied. "I thought that for a second, then I realised he was just appraising my diamonds."

The Secret Service agents began to clear the room. Megan kissed me goodbye and wished me luck with my speech. I was alone at the bar when I saw the president of the United States for the first time. He was standing in the corner on his own, looking a little awkward. He spotted me and recognized me at the same time. He walked over with that huge goofy smile of his, a weird moment in my life rivalled only by the day I was chased by what I assumed to be killer ducks during a horrible acid trip.

"Good day, Craig. "How are you?" asked the free world's leader, extending a cordial hand.

I had dreamt about what I would say to the president if I had a private conversation with him for months before the event. Would I chastise him for everything he had done that I so strongly opposed, chastise him for his foreign policy, his Middle East strategy, his disrespect for the Kyoto Protocol and the Geneva Conventions? Would I persuade him to change his mind about education, the economy, and the drug war, and then remind him of the constitutional requirement to keep church and state separate? Finally, I determined that lecturing the president of the United States about the constitution of his own country might be a little arrogant. After all, he'd previously been attacked by some very sophisticated politicians and journalists, many of whom were far more and more informed than an uneasy vaudevillian in an ill-fitting tuxedo. However, I couldn't pass up the opportunity to express my displeasure, so I threw caution to the wind and charged him with biting...

"Hello, sir, nice to meet you."

He startled me and disarmed me since he was not what I expected. I'd seen much too much MSNBC and was expecting to meet a drooling fool.

I told him I was going to slam the press as much as the politicians, and he appeared relieved.

After all, he was already a lame-duck president viewed as an election liability by his own party, with a lower approval rating than many expected. Attacking him too aggressively would be the equivalent of joining a fight after it had ended and declaring victory.

I decided to handle the situation like the legendary Christmas Day episode from World War I, when German and British forces took a day break from killing each other and played soccer in no-man's land.

I asked former WHCA dinner speakers Jay Leno and Drew Carey what they did when they were there, and they both gave me identical advice. Read the room, don't be too blue but also don't be too tame, whack everyone at least once, and remember that it's not about you, you're just the help.

I spoke briefly about why I became an American, without cursing, and when I finished, they gave me a standing ovation, so I can only infer that my method succeeded.

I don't think I was particularly shining that night; I believe the audience was simply as pleased as I was that the whole affair was over and nothing too humiliating had occurred.

After that, everything was a blur. Backslapping and schmoozing with celebs. I felt like an anvil had been taken from the top of my head. Megan and I arrived in our room about three a.m. and had to get up at six a.m. to catch our flight back to Los Angeles.

That I became a citizen of this nation in January and attended a dinner with the president in March is, I believe, evidence that we are still the country we wish to be. I'd wanted to be an American citizen for a long time; I'd felt like an American since I was thirteen and first travelled here. Life got in the way, or, to be more precise, I got in my own way. My personal issues got in the way, but America is the nation of the second, third, and 106th chances. As I drifted off on the farty rattly jet on the way home, I reflected about my brief talk with the president.

We were talking about Scotland; he had travelled there when he was younger and expressed puzzled wonder at the amount of drinking that was done there, implying that he had participated to a significant degree. We briefly discussed the hazards of alcohol. I've been sober for seventeen years, and rumour has it that he's been sober even longer.

"It's a long way from where I've been standing here talking to the president," I said to him.

"It's a long way from where I could've ended up to being the president," he said.

"Only in America," he remarked, laughing.

We clinked our sparkling water glasses.

"Damn straight, Mr. President," that's what I said.

And I have faith in it.

Chapter 2: Frank Sinatra and Elizabeth Taylor

It most likely started when the Germans attempted to murder my parents. Every night, when the weather permitted, the Germans would fly over in their Heinkels and Messerschmitts and dump bombs on Glasgow, only a few miles from where my parents grew up. My father was ten years old at the time, and my mother was seven, but the Jerries didn't care; they needed to crush Glasgow since it was the British Empire's military workshop. All of the battleships, minesweepers, and frigates that would be used to put an end to Fascism were being built at the vast, filthy shipyards that some idiot had erected just next to my home. So, every night they could, the Germans sought to assassinate everybody who stood in their path. My parents never forgiven them for the nightly assaults that claimed the lives of several of their classmates. My mother and father always referred to them as "Germans," never "Nazis." That sounded too impersonal and heartless, which I believe it was; however, by naming the adversary Germans, it helped my parents to keep the enmity alive, and if you know anything about Scottish people, you know that holding a grudge is something we excel at.

When the American GIs arrived in Glasgow on their way to Europe, their white teeth and lack of rickets must have made them seem like gods.

They also brought goods that had been forgotten since the beginning of the war. Fruit, nylons, laughter, and hope. With America embroiled in the war, my parents' generation realised that it would eventually finish and that life would continue on. Perhaps things would get even better if the GIs brought something else. Something that had to be there before I could exist. Swing dancing is a type of dance.

Even now, every Friday and Saturday night in Glasgow, pubs and bars are full with young people pounding down as much Dutch courage as they can before heading out for radancin to meet potential sexual partners or future wives. That's how my parents met, just like thousands of other Glaswegians.

When I was younger, my father, Bob, was rake thin, but he was tall and good-looking, and at six-one, he was a giant for a Scotsman of his generation. Diamond-blue eyes, white-blonde hair that had turned silver by his thirties, a powerful nose, and fantastic teeth, but the teeth were a bit of a cheat because they were dentures. Bob informed me he'd lost his own teeth when he was flung from his Enfield dispatch motorcycle at Anderston Cross while speeding at eighty miles per hour, but this seems unlikely because: no one can get eighty miles per hour out of a 1945 Enfield dispatch motorcycle.

Nonetheless, the Great Teeth Incident has become family folklore, which is fine with me, but the more likely version is that my father lost his teeth at a young age as a result of his genuinely Dickensian childhood diet. He didn't own shoes until he was eleven years old, and he was evacuated from the inner city to one of the notorious childhood labour workhouses-sweatshops in the countryside that kept children safe from bombs but not from horrifying abuse and mistreatment at the hands of wartime opportunists for a few years during the war. My father refused to discuss the specifics of his military experience until the day he died, saying simply that it was not enjoyable. I trusted him.

I also thought he rode a motorcycle and rode it rapidly. After all, he was a telegraph delivery kid in Glasgow in the early 1950s, around the time Marlon Brando played a tormented and gloomy motorcycle gang member in The Wild One.

It's seen in antique images. Her hair was raven black, and her eyes were the colour of Celtic coral. She was lush and slightly zaftig, a lovely, intelligent young lady, which I suppose made her a target for jealousy and contempt from others who were not genetically fortunate. It must have been terrible and humiliating for her, and my mother inevitably acquired a hardness, a shell to defend herself with. I believe she had to hide her genius in order to compensate for her appearance, which eventually made her angry. Netta resembled Elizabeth Taylor, but she was tougher.

Their relationship had always eluded me. They seemed to quarrel a lot when I was younger, and even their adoration was veiled in little passive-aggressive insults that they would transmit through their children. "Yer faither disnae like my cookin'," he says in front of us, maybe during dinner. That's why he's making that expression."

"Aye, yer mother disnae like yer father, that's why she's makin' that face."

And then our parents would laugh in a weird sad manner, and we kids would laugh just because they were laughing, but I still have no idea what was going on.

Netta worked just as hard to keep the house and study to become a grade school teacher so she could bring home extra money and give herself a sense of purpose after her own children left. My parents' problems were not the same as mine. Their adversary was poverty, not the "Oh shit, we can't afford cable" kind, but the "Oh shit, we can't afford food" kind. So they tried their best for their family, despite having little time for emotional connection. It was as if too many public demonstrations of affection were a luxury reserved for the wealthy or the English. Add to that the impact, if modest in my home, of sterile Scottish

The first openly passionate moment I watched between my parents-- not to suggest they didn't have them; after all, they had four kids-- occurred right before my father's death. It wasn't so much the freshness of the moment that surprised me as the overwhelming sense that it wasn't novel for them at all. This was not the first time these two people had experienced anything similar. It is a testament to my own selfishness and self-obsession that I was previously unaware of.

Netta would bring him boiled sweets, magazines, and whatever else he wanted from home. She was so intent on him that I don't think she was always aware of my sisters, brother, and myself being in the same room with them. She simply sat on his bed and massaged his hair. (Even rigorous chemo couldn't take his magnificent hair away; it only turned limp and downy.) On one of her trips, I observed as my parents locked eyes and dad muttered something to her that only they could hear, and she chuckled a little and kissed him on the lips.

On the tongue.

They appeared to be young and in love.

He was like Frank Sinatra, and she was like Elizabeth Taylor.

Chapter 3: The Attic

On May 17, 1962, at 6:10 a.m., I was born in Stobhill Hospital in Springburn, near Glasgow's northern outskirts. My parents drove me home a few days later to the modest rented apartment a short bus ride from the hospital, where my brother and sister awaited. My parents had already filed for and been awarded government accommodation in the new town of Cumbernauld, so I only resided there for six months.

Following World War II, Glasgow had to rehouse a massive number of people. Bombing had severely devastated the town, and many of the tenement houses had fallen into disrepair as a result of slum landlording and urban poverty. A generation of architects and engineers had been inspired by the promise of a "New Dawn" and a peaceful economic revival in the 1950s. They had plans for the commons. Housing schemes--vast expanses of cheap matchbox houses with none of the attendant comforts of city life, such as a cinema, a store, or a library, just miles of dreary towers built on the outskirts of town. They resembled projects on the fringes of Moscow or East Berlin, with the extra bonus of the damp Scottish environment to up the suffering ante.

These tragedies were planned by pseudointellectual modernists who assumed that by the 1970s, the automobile will have replaced feet. Any money left over from building boxlike living hutches was spent on hideous concrete abstract sculptures, totems to the gods of complete banality, which were scattered throughout the town. Because there were no sidewalks, people were diverted into tunnels coated with corrugated iron (a cheap way to construct them) to avoid interfering with automobile flow on the empty freeways. As the new towns fell, the tunnels became useful for gang fighting and glue sniffing.

The Cumbernauld town planners probably never saw the finished product, but I'm sure it looked a lot better as line drawings on expensive paper. Cumbernauld was recently ranked the second-worst town in the United Kingdom, trailing only the city of Hull, a drab seaport on England's east coast. I disagree with the outcome; I've been to Hull, and while it is undeniably a shithole, it is no match for Cumbernauld.

Lynn was born when I was three years old. I was sent to my grandmother's house while my mother was expecting and giving birth to my younger sister. She was apparently abroad for some time due to a tough pregnancy.

Nobody explained where my mother had gone because of my family's aversion to sex. She was admitted to the hospital with "women's trouble," which means nothing to a three-year-old. Because the hospital had a bizarre rule prohibiting small children from visiting the maternity wards, family legend has it that I got an eye infection from standing and staring at my grandmother's mailbox for hours on end in the hope that my mother would return. In my family, this is regarded as a humorous anecdote. It's a miracle I'm not in solitary confinement eating spiders and yelling curses at my testicles.

I was irritated when my mother eventually returned home with my infant sister. She was a whiny little fartball who always stole my thunder, but she grew up to be one of the funniest people I know, despite the fact that she can still be farty and whiney.

She now works as a writer on my TV show, which I shamelessly exploit for my own gain. Sweet vengeance.

The family had grown to six people, and while my parents must have been struggling financially, the kids were never aware of it. I knew we couldn't afford many luxuries, but neither could anyone else. It's not like we lived in Beverly Hills. In fact, when we had our hallway carpeted--a terrifying vomity-coloured tweedish patterned stuff donated by a friend of my father's who worked in the shipyards and received a piece from a luxury liner--neighbours came from all around to marvel at its great grandeur.

The attic was fantastic. It was barely the size of a cupboard but big enough to house four kids and some toys, and it was set aside for the kids' sole use. We jammed ourselves in there for hours and hours, hours that lasted years. We were arguing, fighting, laughing, and playing in the attic. Experiments could be conducted away from the harsh parental gaze. My brother and I used a cheap chemical set to make the worst scent in the world, which has yet to be surpassed in my view. My brother told me that the game of darts was played with one person throwing the darts while the other held the board, therefore I still have a scar on my leg. I was the one in charge.

Janice eventually stopped coming. She was in high school, liked pop music, and suddenly seemed to despise the rest of us. Scott, her year younger, then followed suit. They told Lynn and me that after we went to bed, which was obviously earlier than they did, the toys in the attic came to life, and that we wouldn't be able to see it until we were older. Lynn and I thought it was just the casual malice of teenage siblings playing on naïve younger siblings.

I believe we still do. Janice and Scott grew up with stable lifestyles and regular salaries. Lynn and I take chances amusing other people, and I'm not sure either of us has truly grown up or left the attic. Lynn, like me, still believes that the toys can communicate.

Chapter 4: Astronaut

I'm not saying this to brag, but I was a bedwetter until I was about eleven years old. Then I came to a halt, but only briefly. I began consuming alcohol on a regular basis in my early teens, after which I returned to intermittent bedwetting until I was twenty-nine. I haven't peed myself since February 18, 1992, the day I became sober. As a result, I believe I was a bedwetter until I was nearly thirty. But I did stop before I was thirty, and I believe my family and the people of Scotland should be very proud of that.

I, too, was a chubby kid. Tubby was my nickname, and I had the usual gaseous discharges of a youngster who gleefully gorged himself on what was deemed nutritious in Scotland in the 1960s--lard and salt. A frightened, overweight, incontinent boy could seem tough to adore, yet it didn't seem to bother my parents at all.

It was a different story for instructors.

She belted me on my first day at Muirfield, an unsightly prefabricated structure that resembled a small, dowdy factory. It was 1967, and I had just turned five years old, but physical punishment remained lawful in Scottish schools until 1979, when it was outlawed by the European Court of Human Rights. It seemed nearly mandatory when I first started school.

When I returned home that day, I told my mother about Mrs. Sherman (first name unknown, but I assumed something harsh like Agnes) and, while I received a reasonably sympathetic hearing, the prevailing attitude was that I had somehow deserved it. (I didn't think so then, and I still don't today, but after forty years, maybe it's time to move on.) My parents came from an age that believed physicians, teachers, and police officers were always correct and would never let you down. They let the teachers beat us because they believed teachers knew best, and my childhood seemed pampered and lovely in comparison to their own.

Fear was the overarching theme of my childhood outside the house from Mrs. Sherman's office. That's what I recall: being terrified. Of course, the teachers terrified me. The other youngsters did as well, but it had to be kept hidden. There was a cruel Darwinism in the schoolyards, albeit it was more about bluff than true fighting until the teen years. Early on, the professors were the only ones who were actually violent. As a result, I learned to bluff. I attempted to appear alternatively aloof and enigmatically menacing, which is no easy accomplishment for an apprehensive, corpulent, farty adolescent, but I made it through. I believe the armour I utilised to survive in Hollywood was forged during the time. Appear stronger, cooler, or funnier than you are, and you have a chance of succeeding.

It was especially dangerous to stand out in any way at school. If you excelled academically, you'd have to pay the price on the playground. I usually made a point of getting a few questions wrong on tests so that I would pass but not by much. You couldn't fail by too much, or else the other kids would mock you for being a stupid. Obviously, you couldn't be a teacher's pet, but being too much of a rebel would be a mistake, because the teaching staff would single you out, and every time they needed someone to belt, it'd be you, guilty or not. In the 1960s and 1970s, the only way to survive a public education in Scotland was to remain nameless. Don't let yourself down. You will not succeed. Don't show up. Simply do not. Any movement could be hazardous. This has the effect of dampening a child's inherent ambition. I surely learnt to keep my mouth quiet about whatever dreams I had. It surprised me later to learn that education was not always like this.

But school did give me one of the most valuable gifts of my life. I learnt to read and will be eternally grateful. Otherwise, I would have died. I read alone as soon as I was able. I sought refuge in literature, whether under the covers with a lantern or in my attic nook. It was through books that I first became aware of the types of jerks I was dealing with. I also discovered comrades in books, individuals my age who were going through or had triumphed over the same nonsense. Tom and Huck had to cope with a lot of injustice, and Huck's pappy looked exactly like one of my teachers. "William" by Richmal Crompton was a cunning and humorous guerilla against adult rule.

This strong sense of loneliness, hatred, misanthropy, and terror in a prepubescent child appears to me today to be an immensely foreboding portent. I should have registered for rehab back then.

When I was seven years old, I was allowed to stay up till one o'clock in the morning one night. My entire family was crowded around the television, including my four-year-old baby sister, and I couldn't understand why she should be permitted to stay up so late when I had never been allowed to at that age. My brother pointed out that I was only seven years old and that he hadn't been permitted to stay up this late (and he was nearly twelve!), so he threw a sock in it.

I posted them above my bed in the room I shared with my older brother, and despite his preference for Raquel Welch in a fur bikini at the time, he admitted my NASA posters were cool. They certainly moved me closer to America, and maybe more importantly, they united me with Gunka James.

Chapter 5: Brick House

Muirfield Primary school was dreadful, but at least the violence was limited to the teachers. Cumbernauld High School, which I started when I was twelve, was a whole new box of crabs for me.

Because of the location of my residence, I was obligated to attend that redbrick prison, despite the fact that all of my confederates--and I use that phrase with a defeated army in mind--were to attend Green-faulds, the town's second protestant high school. For Catholics, there was also Our Lady's. Only Catholics are allowed.

Cumbernauld High School had a large student body in the mid-1970s, with about three thousand students ranging in age from twelve to eighteen. It was only required to attend school until the age of sixteen, but anyone hoping for a university education or even a competent trade had to stay for another two years. Needless to say, the thugs and losers went at sixteen, so you were in clover if you could make it through the first four years. People commented on how tiny the lessons were and how the teachers were less jumpy and belthappy. I wouldn't know because I've never been that far.

I was afraid from the first day I arrived. Nobody in my class had gone to Muirfield, and I didn't know anyone. It rapidly became clear that I was the nephew of a teacher--Gunka James to me, Mr. Ingram to them--putting me in an incredibly vulnerable position, though I never knew if this was because my uncle was on the staff or if it would have been worse if he hadn't been. I believe it was a little of both, depending on whether I was dealing with a teacher or a student.

Of course, my older brother and sister were already at school, but there was no assistance. They had filled my mind with nasty fantasies about Big Jimmy, the assistant headmaster, who, according to my siblings, could belt so loudly that students ended up in the hospital or their hair turned white with shock. As it turned out, nonsense. Big Jimmy had an arm, but it was one of the better ones.

I gradually became acquainted with the thirty or so students in my class. We were obliged to sit wherever the teacher wanted us to sit in any particular class as we walked from lesson to lesson. Soon, a pecking order was developed, which was completely inappropriate in today's opinion. For boys, popularity was determined solely by perceived toughness; for girls, it was determined solely by appearance. The system gradually evolved into something slightly more civilised, but that was it for the first few months.

The brawl began in science class, taught by Mr. Weir, a quiet ghoul with a lightning-fast lashing technique. Ronnie Souter indicated that I was a gay because my uncle was a maths teacher in order to impress Maxine Hawthorne, the raven haired class beauty. I stated unequivocally that Ronnie was significantly more likely to be gay, given that he dressed like a member of the Bay City Rollers--a condition over which he probably had some influence. Maxine burst out laughing. Ronnie was flushed. The challenge had been issued.

I was left with bruising and a horrible shiner on my face. However, this was 1975. That year, I would get a considerably bigger poke in the eye.

The following one arrived from America.

Chapter 6: The Filth and the Fury

When I did drink again, it was not El-D, and I was cautious, consuming only a few beers before going to the Y disco, and I quickly saw why everyone was so excited about alcohol: it was enjoyable. If you had the appropriate buzz, you could feel like a giant as you walked into the darkened church hall where the females were already dancing in tiny circles about their handbags.

The Y disco was run by a well-meaning but realistic social worker named Stuart, I believe. It appears that half of Scotland's population is named Stuart, with the majority of them being men. YStuart was one of those humanitarian poet types created by a middle-class upbringing and a liberal education. Y-Stuart truly desired to live in Cumbernauld in order to assist local teenagers. He was a truly wonderful man, but we thought he was unusual and vilified him amongst ourselves as a predatory paederast, which he was not. He did, however, have some weird ideas. Once inside the hall, Y-Stuart granted all of the teenagers full rein. He didn't stop people from kissing or fighting; he just let it happen. He'd call the cops if things got out of hand, but they never did. We all knew that if the cops were called too frequently, the club would be closed down, which no one wanted. Y-Stuart did not allow everyone to enter the hall. He'd insist on smelling your breath first, thinking that was the only way to tell if you'd been drinking or using glue, the only other mood enhancer accessible. Glue sniffing was quite popular among a select group of people at the time. It would be a few years before the British working classes discovered hashish, which would come in cheap and plentiful supply from Afghanistan, Pakistan, and Lebanon, and it would be a long time before heroin arrived and brought the whole fucking thing down a notch. In the mid-1970s, kids looking to get high would purchase a bag of potato chips and a tube of Evo-Stick. They'd consume or throw away the chips, then squeeze the glue into the empty chip bag, cover their mouth and nose with the bag, and inhale the contents deeply, fast, and frequently. The hallucinogenic impact was quickly followed by a strangely ethereal, giggly buzz, but with the unfortunate side effect of occasionally murdering individuals. It was considered low-rent, so only the true wackos did it.

In those days, the music my friends and I listened to seemed incidental to dancing with or glancing at girls. It was merely background noise, the same old nonsense that had been going on for years. Every Thursday night on Top of the Pops, we'd see the usual bouffant-haired crooners in bedazzled jumpsuits singing about Mandy, Boogaloo, Rainbows, and other nonsense, accompanied by session guys playing Fender Rhodes keyboards. Of course, there was some good stuff. Everyone adored Bowie, but his songs about aliens seemed odd, and he was far too effete for us at the time.

We'd been hearing about the Sex Pistols on the news and in the newspapers, this crazy London band whose nasty behaviour was offending everyone. This was a call to arms for a teen lad. Here were folks with whom I could identify. They didn't have vehicles, money, girlfriends, or anything else, and they were upset. Perfect.

The Damned were the first punk rock band I heard, not the Pistols. I heard their double-A-side single "New Rose/ Neat Neat Neat" at Craig Keaney's place after school, and it was an incredible and dramatic surprise, even with the level turned down because his father was sick. The energy and sound were combative. It was exhilarating and wonderful. Punk had come, and I was on board.

Our parents and instructors detested punk, which added to its appeal. By the summer of 1977, I was leaving my house in the evenings to hang out on street corners with my buddies, spitting and smoking. My parents forbade me from wearing the painted tattered uniform that declared my devotion, so every night I went to my hidden hideout beneath the highway bridge near my house to change in plain view of old ladies riding the buses that trundled by. Many children followed a similar regimen. Everyone had their own tiny hideaway where they could transform into their punk alter ego. We referred to it as getting "punked up." We, too, had punk names: Davie Vomit, Johnny Shite, and Harry Bastard. Adam Eternal was chosen because my great grandpa Adam perished in World War I, and I thought the word "eternal" sounded fascinating.

We would sulk on the sidelines of the Y-Disco dressed as our nihilistic heroes from the London punk scene until the DJ (Stuart again) played a punk record, at which point all the girls would flee and the punky boys like me would rush the dance floor to do our punk dances, which were the Pogo-standing very straight with your arms glued to your sides then jumping up and down, as if heading an invisible soccer ball-or the Dead Fly

I wanted to dye my hair, but it would have gotten me belted and made me stand out too much from the other kids, inviting a kicking. My peers had not all embraced the new wave of music and design. I read somewhere that food dyes could be used to colour hair temporarily, so I went to the kitchen cupboard where my mother kept ingredients for her infrequent forays into baking fairy cakes or clootie dumplings (a rich fruit cake popular in Scotland). I didn't find any food dye, but I did find a small bottle of vanilla extract. Because vanilla ice cream is blond, I reasoned that vanilla flavouring would have the same effect on hair. I shampooed it in, and nothing occurred except that I smelt fantastic and was chased around by every dog in the neighbourhood for nearly a month.

I started or joined a plethora of various but always terrible bands with names like Night Creatures, the News, Prussia (what the fuck!), and the Fast Colours. Truly pitiful outfits that would practise in garages. They were truly garage bands, with the one kid crowbarred into the group despite playing a hopelessly inappropriate instrument (flute/oboe/accordion) because his father owned a car and was ready to bring our instruments to practise. Until you hear "Anarchy in the

U.K." with a clarinet solo, you haven't heard it butchered.

It was an incredible and dramatic realisation for someone who was sick. The energy and sound were combative. It was exhilarating and wonderful. Punk had come, and I was on board.

Our parents and instructors detested punk, which added to its appeal. By the summer of 1977, I was leaving my house in the evenings to hang out on street corners with my buddies, spitting and smoking. My parents forbade me from wearing the painted tattered uniform that declared my devotion, so every night I went to my hidden hideout beneath the highway bridge near my house to change in plain view of old ladies riding the buses that trundled by. Many children followed a similar regimen. Everyone had their own tiny hideaway where they could transform into their punk alter ego. We referred to it as getting "punked up." We, too, had punk names: Davie Vomit, Johnny Shite, and Harry Bastard. Adam Eternal was chosen because my great grandpa Adam perished in World War I, and I thought the word "eternal" sounded fascinating.

We would sulk on the sidelines of the Y-Disco dressed as our nihilistic heroes from the London punk scene until the DJ (Stuart again) played a punk record, at which point all the girls would flee and the punky boys like me would rush the dance floor to do our punk dances, which were the Pogo-standing very straight with your arms glued to your sides then jumping up and down, as if heading an invisible soccer ball-or the Dead Fly

I wanted to dye my hair, but it would have gotten me belted and made me stand out too much from the other kids, inviting a kicking. My peers had not all embraced the new wave of music and design. I read somewhere that food dyes could be used to colour hair temporarily, so I went to the kitchen cupboard where my mother kept ingredients for her infrequent forays into baking fairy cakes or clootie dumplings (a rich fruit cake popular in Scotland). I didn't find any food dye, but I did find a small bottle of vanilla extract. Because vanilla ice cream is blond, I reasoned that vanilla flavouring would have the same effect on hair. I shampooed it in, and nothing occurred except that I smelt fantastic and was chased around by every dog in the neighbourhood for nearly a month.

I started or joined a plethora of various but always terrible bands with names like Night Creatures, the News, Prussia (what the fuck!), and the Fast Colours. Truly pitiful outfits that would practise in garages. They were truly garage bands, with the one kid crowbarred into the group despite playing a hopelessly inappropriate instrument (flute/oboe/accordion) because his father owned a car and was ready to bring our instruments to practise. Until you hear "Anarchy in the U.K." with a clarinet solo, you haven't heard it butchered.

Meanwhile, the London scene soon transitioned from punk to the heinous New Romantic period, with bands like Culture Club, Spandau Ballet, Duran Duran, and the absolutely heinous Visage, but we were a little behind the curve and happily stayed pure a little longer.

The attitude was as important as the music. That sanctimonious, whimpering sixties mob with their Love and Peace and dubious tolerance of folk music deserves a real fuck-you. Punk rock seemed to belong to us, with no rules and no leaders. It was complete chaos, and I loved it. I knew it was an immature adolescent fantasy at the time, but I didn't care; I was an immature adolescent fantasist. It was perfect for me.

Obviously, my new worldview caused me to have genuine troubles at school, but I discovered a solution.

I left.

Chapter 7: The Real World

My parents were startled and frightened by my decision to drop out of school at sixteen, the youngest age allowed by the state. My older sister, Janice, and my brother, Scott, had gone on to higher education, with Scott even moving out of the house--he decided he wanted to be a journalist and took a flat with a bunch of mock hippies in Glasgow's unfashionable (and thus fashionable to some students) Denniston area. Scott worked at the University of Strathclyde during the week and did his laundry on weekends. Janice, now a young scientist, commuted to the same university from the family home every day on the same nonstop bus that I had taken with Gunka James.

Over the years, I've attempted to figure out why my siblings did better in school than I did, but I've never found a good answer. They obviously kept company with the same professors and students and were surrounded by the same violence and threats, but they managed to traverse it all with far greater ease. Lynn, my younger sister, claims it was just as difficult for her as it was for me.

My mother believed that my loud voice made me a visible target. When I was ten years old and being harassed by a hideous old harpy of a teacher named Mrs. White, my mother tried to teach me whispering so that Mrs. White wouldn't notice me as much. I believe the real reason was that I was a needy little cur who craved attention, and in my environment, if you were noticed, you got whacked.

I did have a love of literature that outweighed my dislike of the individuals who taught it, and I believe that because I had no respect for the teachers, their attitude did not taint the writing that I was discovering for myself. That makes me happy. I've often spoken with well-educated men and women who despise the classics because they were forced to read them. This is something I understand. Nobody made me read Crime and Punishment. I read it on my own volition. I didn't write a paper about it, but I found it interesting and thought-provoking. I was shocked at how much I identified with Raskolnikov's whiny self-justification--clearly, there was a warning here.

I believe in education, and I sometimes wish, generally when an embarrassing gap in my knowledge emerges during a conversation with a well-educated person, that I had somehow managed to remain with my schooling and pursue a road into an organised college or university degree, but I didn't. But, most of the time, I believe that being an autodidact--a dilettante, if you will--has given me as much as it has taken away.

I had no notion what I was going to do for a living once I graduated from high school. I wanted to be a rock star, hailed and admired and worshipped, drunk, bedded, stunning, and dead by the age of twenty-five, but it was too Byronic and romantic for a Protestant, working-class guy, so I put that dream on hold for a while and pursued something comparable but more within my financial means. I started working as an apprentice electrician.

Joining the adult world had some unexpected consequences. On the manufacturing floor, I met Bert, a short, bearded American who had served in Vietnam before fleeing the country in disgust because of how he was treated when he returned. His rage-filled journey through Europe eventually led him to Scotland, where he met and married a redhead girl. Bert told me about drugs, Vietnam, the Summer of Love, San Francisco, and Los Angeles, and you could tell he missed America despite his cynicism.

I met Alex, a man who had polio as a child and had to walk with sticks and leg braces. He drove a three-wheeled blue automobile provided by the government for disabled people and smoked the best hashish in Scotland. He'd obtain some for you as well, because cops never stopped a disabled vehicle. Willie was also introduced to me.

Acid was insane. Whenever I went on an acid trip, which I believe I took maybe twenty or thirty times before the age of twenty-one, I always believed it lasted far too long. The insane giggling, the otherworldliness, the useless insights. It had just outstayed its welcome. Always. Anyone who has consumed acid will understand what I mean. It's dreadful, and when you have a poor experience--a bad trip--it's hellacious. The last time I used acid, I had a rough trip, but it wasn't until much later, when I was chased by savage yet largely fictional killer ducks in Kelvingrove Park in Glasgow. There was no crack because it hadn't yet become available, but there was some opium, which we smoked in a bong. And, of course, there was heroin--"You gotta at least try it, man"--at some point.

I was never a fan of heroin. I tried it a few times, but it made me nauseated and sleepy, and I needed to eat. This irritated my fellow users since they felt sick and thought it was inappropriate to order pizza when you were on the nod. I thought it was hypocritical to give us rules while we were high on heroin, but I guess even junkies have their rules. I never shot smack (thank God), but instead sucked the fumes from a smouldering line set out on tinfoil, a practice known as "chasing the dragon" in the absurdly melodramatic lexicon of opiate addicts. Even sober addicts frequently refer to themselves as dope fiends, as if smoking heroin made you scarier and more "out there" than a blackout drunk. Addicts can be fiercely competitive about their misery.

Another reason I never tried heroin was because of the people around me who did. They were all so self-righteously corrupt. They reminded me of my little pal Raskolnikov. I would have definitely gone into further problems with Willie and his pharmaceutical buffet, but then I met Gillian, and it was not the last time I was saved by love. My two big loves in life.

Women and booze.

Chapter 8: Love and Sex

The concept that any normal female would actually want to have sex was regarded as nonsense by my peers. We'd been told from a young age that sex was terrible and awful, that men craved it constantly because they were slaves to their appetites, and that women were good, that they didn't want or desire sex but would let it in order to produce babies, or because they were drunk, or because they were English. No one said it out loud; it was just hinted at. I received no sexual education in school, and there was never any "talk" from my parents, so I am also an autodidact in that area. I believe I approached my academics with zeal and enthusiasm unrivalled in other areas of my life.

If I wanted to be near Gillian, I had to give up the drugs, which was not an issue for me because I genuinely wanted to be around Gillian. Before meeting Gillian, all the girls I had kissed or messed around with were not people I was drawn to; they were simply available and willing to put up with my breathy attempts at sexy. She was stunning. Voluptuous and captivating, like a young Loren, with deep, dark-brown eyes and hair as shining as the shampoo commercials on TV. She smelled faintly of peaches and had no sign of acne on her skin. I met her at a party shortly after dropping out of school and began communicating with her. I asked if I could accompany her home, and she agreed. She also said she couldn't be my girlfriend because she was going on vacation with her parents the next day and possibly meeting someone, but I didn't care. It was a warm, summer night, and I wanted to spend as much time as possible with her. I walked her back to her house; she lived in a nice neighbourhood near the other protestant school she had attended. I was standing outside her front door when she kissed me firmly on the lips, and I could sense her desire, not as a favour or a blessing, but as something she desired. I was stunned and perplexed, but before I could even think about going upstairs, she had said goodbye and gone inside, leaving me breathless on her doorstep.

On the way home, I ran into some of my friends. "Just winching," I explained, but they didn't seem to mind. Even merely winning someone who resembled Gillian was a success.

She was gone for three weeks. Her family had a small budget and had taken their annual holiday to the seemingly exotic locale of San Francisco. I tried not to think of her having sex with big-toothed American boys, but it was difficult. I'd been there, I'd seen the promised dental land.

That night, she arrived before me. I'd been drinking hard cider and Breaker malt liquor in the woods with some Stuart or other beforehand, but I wasn't drunk, just buzzed enough to be confident. When I arrived at the party, someone told me she was in the kitchen with some other girls. I walked in to say hello and nearly passed out. She had a rich golden tan that added to her lusciousness. I asked if she had a good time.

Funny, but I had a feeling she wouldn't. After all, it was San Francisco; if you're a guy worried about the female you adore hooking up with someone on her trip, I think San Francisco is the safest bet, assuming she doesn't give her heart to a lesbianand who among us hasn't?

We stayed in Romford with my Uncle Davie and Aunt Sylvia. We visited Big Ben and the Houses of Parliament, as well as other tourist attractions. We were in love, and Uncle Davie and Aunt Sylvia let us sleep in the same room during our trip. They assumed we were allowed to do so in Scotland, and while this was not the case, Gillian and I stayed quiet about it. We had a lot of fun in Scotland, but the trip to London was when we fully committed to each other. We had lost our virginity to one another.

We were both seventeen at the time, and our relationship was wonderfully comfortable, safe, and romantic, but by the time I was nineteen, the momentum of our love had taken over, and I felt stuck. There was discussion of an engagement, and I thought I'd be with her for the rest of my life, but if it came down to Gillian vs America, she'd lose. We went to a birthday celebration in Glasgow's Rock Garden one night.

Their sound was thrilling, rough, fantastic, spooky, and loud. Similar to the Cramps, but stranger. Peter Capaldi, their lead singer, had the most imposing stage presence I'd ever seen. He declared at the end of the set that this would be the band's final show because they couldn't find a permanent drummer.

That was the end of Gillian and me.

Chapter 9: A Clever and Patient Monster

In my life, I've spoken to a lot of people. I've read a lot of books, seen a lot of movies and plays, and heard a lot of opinions on a wide range of subjects, but no subject has given me more misinformed random garbage than alcoholism. Alcoholism, to me, is similar to Los Angeles: everyone believes they've been there and know the town because they've seen Entourage or visited Disneyland, but only those who have lived there for a few years truly understand. This is how alcoholism works. If you drank a few too many beers in college, blacked out, or fell off a bar stool, you don't know anything about it. Even those who have suffered from alcoholism for years are unable to fathom it if they continue to drink, and those who have recovered from this seemingly hopeless state of mind and body appear to agree on only a few points. It's devious. It's perplexing. It is both forceful and patient.

People still ask me how much I drank every day, and I honestly don't know. I didn't keep a diary. Because it wasn't Weight Watchers, there was no tally sheet. Every day, I drank what I had to. That was the amount of alcohol I consumed. And now comes the tricky part. It is not sequential. I didn't drink every day till the very end. I could never predict or even estimate what I would do after just one sip of booze.

Then it might stop for a few hours, or even days. Exactly like that. I slept, I didn't drink with the same zeal, and I started to feel a little more human. It came back almost as abruptly. I had no idea when the terror would come. In the car, on the bus, or in bed. I used to wake up screaming every now and then. I sensed something was going on inside of me that I couldn't control. It could be medicated and calmed with alcohol, but one of the adverse effects was that when I woke up, the terror would be stronger. It's a vicious circle. Many people have asked me why I didn't seek help since then, but the fact is that I didn't know what was wrong with me. "This is just who I am, a terrorised man, a lunatic, a neurotic," I reasoned, and I reasoned that the only way out was to preserve some outward pretence of normalcy or else I'd be put up forever in a padded cell. Internally, I was in a state of near-constant fear.

The rest of us worked hard to stay friends. For a short while, we even formed another band called the Guests, but Peter's heart was no longer in it. He wanted to be in movies, and Roddy wanted to return to the Western Isles to live with his own hobbit-like island people, so it bled out quickly. Peter made an effort to incorporate me in his new world of actors and filmy types, but I was envious of his success and refused to be pleased with him. Instead, I chose to feel patronised by him. I had nothing to do without band practice, so I went on the dole and drank as much as I could with my unemployment cheque. Tricia arrived at my flat one night and discovered me passed out in bed with another woman, so she poured a bucket of ice water over us. She accurately concluded that her life would be better if she didn't waste any more time on me and went on.

I found myself in the first of the free-falls. "When did you hit rock bottom?" sober alkies are frequently asked, but a more educated query may be, "How many times did you hit rock bottom?"

I had no job, no band, no girlfriend, and no restraints on my behaviour for the first time since leaving school. I was still living in the big flat with Temple; the Dreamboys bassist and I would return there inebriated and angry at all hours of the night with all kinds of people, sometimes even more nasty than myself. Temple and I had no love now that we were no longer bandmates, and he had all the authority because his name was on the lease.

He suggested--quite well, I should add--that I leave and never return.

Of course, he did it joyfully.

Chapter 10: Tripping

During my two years tubthumping with the Dreamboys, I gained buddies. I'd played in other bands, recorded demos, and worked as a session musician on a single or two. As a regular on Glasgow's alternative-rock circuit, I had plenty of places to crash for a few days. A couch in a shared flat, the floor of a friend's room, and occasionally the warm bed of a nice barmaid who should have known better. I would occasionally return to Cumbernauld and swindle cash, food, and laundry services from my parents, but this didn't set well with me. When I was there, I felt like a failure, and my family's obvious worry for me made me nervous.

My reputation as a wild drunk really aided me in gaining employment with other bands. It was true in punk music, as in other areas of show business, that poor behaviour was frequently encouraged rather than condemned. A dipsomaniac train wreck drummer was just what some bands were seeking for. I joined On a Clear Day, a campy, artsy group that was gaining popularity. Their singer was a flamboyant queen, which was unusual, much alone and bold, in Glasgow at the time.

I became good friends with the bassist Robbie McFadyen, a rickety-thin fellow alike who loved to party just as much as I did and had a stronger constitution for it. With his coat on, he must have weighed less than 150 pounds, yet Robbie could drink anyone under the table, and on the few occasions when he passed out in front of me, I could simply toss the man over my shoulder and carry him home. Unfortunately for Robbie, he had to do a lot more for me than I did for him, but fortunately for me, his small stature masked a wonderful power.

He was about ten years older than me and had his life a little more together at thirty. He worked part-time waiting tables at the Spaghetti Factory, a trendy West End restaurant popular with illiterate gastronomes. People who would order a giraffe of red wine to go with their spag bol.

The two straight men went to Robbie's room to avoid sleeping together and having sex. Ken gave me a knowing glance from his perch atop the mantelpiece, and I nodded in agreement before returning to my opiate-induced trance.

After Colin had sneaked out in the morning, Robbie told me that, while nothing had transpired, he suspected Colin was gay.

"Even though he works on the oil rigs?" I inquired.

There was a slight beat. Then we both laughed, Robbie sobbed a little, and he was out, and that was the end of it.

On one especially memorable evening, I even had a brief affair with a guy named Stu. He had handled the Dreamboys for a time, but I didn't realise he was gay until he sat next to me in Bennetts, a notorious club Robbie had taken me to. We were catching up and reminiscing about the amazing times we had with the Dreamboys when Stu abruptly clamped his enormous scaly lips on my face and plunged his massive tongue into my mouth. I nearly peed my pants. I pulled him away, and I recall how astonished he was, but I'm sure I was more surprised. I also recall feeling physically uncomfortable when the bristle on his chin brushed up against mine, and I'm still plagued and scared out by it. My gay male pals have had similar feelings regarding exploratory physical interactions with women.

Stu called me a cock teaser, expecting me to be offended. The strange thing is, I was.

When the guitarist discovered I was shagging his girlfriend, a slender, bright girl named Jill, who also managed the band, I was sacked from On a Clear Day. For a short period, she and I shared a cramped apartment, and while the sex was flamboyant and athletic, she was older than me, and I believe she desired something more. For example, intimacy, and I was a long way from being capable of anything like that. I moved out when she dumped me.

Despite the fact that I'd been kicked out of the band, Robbie and I stayed close, and to help me get over Jill's split, he brought us a couple tabs of acid one Saturday night. We put the little pink pyramid tablets in a pub about a half-hour before it closed, which was eleven p.m. back then. We were driving home across Kelvingrove Park's gothic vastness just as the acid started to kick in. It was intense--I'd tripped many times before but never experienced anything like this. The Victorian statues on the tree-lined streets were staring at us, the wind in the branches was muttering vague frightening warnings, and enigmatic ripples rose up from the plethora of gloomy ornamental ponds. For some reason, Robbie kept changing into Adam Ant. I implored him to stop, but he said that he couldn't. Terror struck like lightning. Then it went away, returned a number of times, and then went quiet again. Then, like a fluorescent light, it turned on and stayed on. Terrifying fear. Robbie felt it as well. We started running, but to our surprise, even at full speed, we were moving painfully slowly. We then heard them. At first a considerable distance away, then behind us and approaching closer.

I went through rainy cobblestone side alleyways, weeping hysterically, until I found myself on Great Western Road, an ancient and vast thoroughfare that leads out of Glasgow to the Highlands. The rain had turned the streets into black mirrors, which was extremely unsettling because they reflected the green of the traffic lights, rendering my entire world green.

I've never been more terrified, lost in a town I know like the back of my hand and on the verge of asphyxiation in a colour.

Then everything turned orange, then red, then green again, and I raced as fast as I could to God knows where.

I returned to the flat, my head zinging and popping but not as awful as earlier. I was terrified and stayed awake for three days afterwards, watching bad TV or staring at Ken. I eventually fell asleep and slept for sixteen hours straight.

I resolved never to do acid again, and I haven't, but just writing about it now, twenty-five years later, makes me feel uneasy and apprehensive, as if I might relapse.

Something should not have transpired within my head that night. I discovered I wasn't bold enough to be insane when acid gave me a clinical, unblinking look at it.

Chapter 11: New York

I married Anne when I was twenty-one years old. She was twenty-six, and both her family and mine had warned her that I was too young and insane to be anyone's husband. My family and her family had also cautioned me that I was too young and insane to imagine I could be anyone's husband. Everyone basically told me that it was a bad idea and that I should abandon it. So, as is customary for me, I vowed to do just that.

He didn't say anything harsh, but rather with sadness, which I understand now that I'm a father. Some mistakes must be tolerated by your children.

The next day, we left for a two-week honeymoon in Amsterdam. Anne liked cannabis and van Gogh, so she thought she'd like it there. She still had a bad hangover from the wedding the night we arrived, so she smoked a massive reefer, which put me in a rage because I had stopped smoking hash following my acid fright and felt everyone else should, too. We battled, she went to bed, and I hung out in the redlight area, getting hammered with a sleazy German dude I met in the hotel bar. That was our honeymoon's first night-Anne passed out alone in the hotel as I drunkenly ogled the whores who displayed their wares in the brothel windows.

However, things improved after that. We made up and spent the rest of our honeymoon in Amsterdam getting wasted together. The French onion soup served in the vast, opulent dining room of the American Hotel in the city centre was a high point for me in two weeks. It is still one of my top 10 soups of all time.

I assisted my uncle with caretaking responsibilities around the estate he now managed for a short while, but I was eager to get into the city. Anne and I rode a train into town one day to meet Jamesy Black, a guy she'd met in Glasgow. He was a fellow art school student who had married an unbelievably beautiful American fashion model named Lucy. They lived on Avenue B between Ninth and Tenth Streets, which was one of New York City's most hazardous districts in the early and mid-1980s.

We met Jamesy in Odessa, that great Avenue A café. I'd never visited the East Village before. I was convinced I'd died and gone to punk-rock heaven. There were Goths, junkies, and rockers mixed in with the terrifying street folks. The entire area seemed to be alive with a physical, cinematic threat. Everywhere I glanced was a movie set--there was real steam rising from the sidewalks, and real Checker cabs were racing down the avenues. The sound of car horns is unlike anywhere else on the planet, as is the scent of New York City--the sweet aroma of pizza mixed with the acidic stench of urine.

The East Village was New York Fuckin' City at its fuckin' best in 1983. My ever-patient Uncle James loaned me $1,000 for the deposit and first month's rent on a little apartment Anne had chosen.

I invested in the equipment and soon found myself earning an astounding $400 per week, tax-free because I was illegal. When a city inspector in a suit arrived at the location, I burst out in a flop sweat, thinking it was the INS. Deportation was the last thing on my mind. I was still persuaded that my future life and happiness lay in America, and that being expelled would make it nearly hard to return.

For a brief moment, it appeared like the insanity of Glasgow's drinking and drugging had finally subsided. Anne and I explored and enjoyed our new surroundings. We saved some money and purchased some necessities for our flat. Jamesy brought us to Rick, the owner of a vintage furniture store on Avenue A, opposite Tompkins Square Park's junked-out no-go zone. Rick was a tubby Englishman who adored 1950s-style plastic chairs and would place them outside his shop. I'm not sure he ever sold anything, but folks liked to hang around there and talk.

There, on the plastic chairs, I met Jamesy's weirdly aloof wife, Lucy, who was a really pretty girl but constantly seemed to be somewhere else. After they split up, Jamesy revealed that she used heroin to lose weight. I met and became friends with Roswell, a little dark-haired Jewish actor from Long Island. Ros was hilarious, but very serious about the craft of acting. He worked on the building site alongside Jamesy and me during the day, but at night he took class after class to develop his sense-memory skills and other such actorly nonsense. He was my favourite.

I ran into pretty much everyone who was anyone in the East Village in the early 1980s at Save the Robots or on the chairs in front of Rick's store. People like Spacely, the legendary one-eyed smack dealer who didn't seem to understand that self promotion and his chosen profession were incompatible, and Grandmaster Flash, a neighbourhood icon on the verge of becoming an international star as one of the founding fathers of the emerging world of rap. I was blown away by his ankle-length gold-lamé coat.

I met Jean-Michel Basquiat, another neighbourhood icon who was being celebrated by Warhol and the New York art world as the daring new face of neo-expressionist American painting at the time. He appeared to be another hazy junkie to me, yet his paintings were and continue to be transcendental in their beauty.

The heroin atmosphere of the neighbourhood rekindled my interest in the drug. When I told Jamesy about it, he informed me that heroin was awful crap, and that there was a far better substance that was cheaper and more fun--and, best of all, it wasn't addictive.

Cocaine.

Chapter 12: Adventures in the Big City

I thought coke was a miracle drug. It allowed you to drink as much as you wanted without passing out or going black. If you took some in the morning, it would cure your hangover and prepare you for a long day of construction labour. It cost sixty dollars a gram, which seemed reasonable given its magical properties. I bought my coke from Jamesy on a daily basis because he had a good coke contact. Anne enjoyed it as well, and while we were far too Presbyterian to go into penury and debauchery over a drug, we made sure to keep it on hand most of the time. Strange as it may seem, cocaine helped at this time--I can only suppose that my relationship with alcohol is so unusual that the introduction of cocaine first relieved the negative consequences. At least, that's how it felt. Of course, it didn't stay that way, but that's how it started.

For a while in New York, I was content. The city's vibrancy and vitality encouraged me and helped me gain confidence, and the East Village streets seemed to be overflowing with people who respected artistic expression and eccentricity. It felt both terrifying and inviting at the same time. Every night at one a.m., while lying in bed, I would hear a woman singing the most beautiful operatic arias. She sounded like an angel flying between the sirens and across the tar roofs. I later discovered that she was an aspiring opera singer who worked in a local pub and would stroll through the streets to her apartment at the end of her shift, screaming at the top of her lungs. She did it for protection, assuming that any bad guys on the street who intended to hurt her would believe she was either insane or would draw too much attention. This both pleased and impressed me. It seemed to reflect the beat of local art as the best defence in a hazardous but thrilling environment.

The auditions were held in the back room, which also served as a dark spot for anonymous gay intercourse during the week and as a classy off-off Broadway theatre on weekends. If you arrive on the wrong night, you may be forced to watch a very amateur version of Our Town when all you wanted was a strange man's penis up your arse.

I sat at the bar and asked the bartender, a very camp black dude named Stanley, for a beer.

I was led inside to meet a tall, skinny, animated figure wearing a purple Donny Osmond cap.

He was sitting behind a small desk in the dark, smokey room, with Peter next to him.

He thought this was lovely and humorous for some reason, so he gave me a screenplay and asked me to read some lines with the Peter Pan fellow, who was an aspiring actor as well as a full-time henchman. Telemachus Clay was the title of the play they were about to stage, written by Lewis John Carlino. It's the story of a farm lad from the Midwest who journeys to Hollywood and seeks forgiveness after a life of dissipation. I played Telemachus, and the Peter Pan impersonator played the manipulative Hollywood agent. I'm not sure how good I was, but I knew Peter Pan was fucking terrible. If this were a competition, I'd be in clover.

I told George that I didn't understand how being in a play would gain me additional construction work.

He informed me that if I wanted to be in show business, which he advocated, people would have to see what I could do. Talent agents and others would attend this production. That explains why there were so many young actors gathered outside.

I explained that I couldn't practise because I had a job.

I was at a loss for what to do, so George gave me a copy of the play and suggested I read it. He'd gather his group at one p.m. the following day, Sunday, and would be overjoyed if I showed there.

I said I'd think about it. I thanked him and walked away.

I met the rest of the cast the next day when I arrived. They were a group of ardent young aspirants, roughly six men and six women, all under the age of twenty-five. George said he was going to "workshop some ideas" and "go through some exercises," whatever that meant, and then make casting decisions.

He made us act out scenes he made up, which always ended with people fighting each other or making love with girls. If this was what it was like to be an actress, I wanted the job. Fuck the money.

Every morning at five a.m., I went to the building site with a breakfast bump of cocaine--by then, it was like coffee to me--and pounded and sawed until three thirty. Then I took the subway back to Harlem, changed, grabbed a slice at Rosemarie's, and rehearsed with the theatrical company until nine o'clock every night. Then I'd yell a couple lines and drink beer till I passed out about midnight. Some nights, I'd travel uptown to meet Anne, who was working in an Irish bar we'll just call O'Tooles because many of the guys I met there respect their anonymity.

If I wanted to chat to Anne, this was my only chance, because otherwise, our only time together was in bed or for an hour or so on weekends, due to our busy schedules. This wasn't as horrible as it sounds because we'd started disagreeing a lot by this point.

I inevitably got to conversing with the other employees who worked there, generally men.Roswell accompanied me to see Anne at O'Tooles one night. We had a few grams of old Bolivian marching powder with us, and she took a few lines but couldn't hang out with us because the restaurant was too crowded and she worked for tips. She seated us in a back booth among Finn, Callum, and a few other Irish transplants. It was one of those evenings when the whiskey and coke flowed like the Mississippi, and after a while, someone recommended we leave the noisy shitheap full of intoxicated yuppies and go to a genuine pub. If Callum and Finn were offended, they didn't show it, and after explaining to Anne that I was going out for a drink with the boys, we all piled into a cab and proceeded to Hell's Kitchen.

I decided to talk these girls out of their chosen vocation with the joyful altruism of a drunk, much to the amusement of Roswell and the assembled Irishmen, who maintained it couldn't be done.

Their pimp interrupted my conversation with the females, who I remember as being giggly and delightful. He was a very tall black man costumed as Huggy Bear. He told me not to bother his host.

I informed him how I felt about his company and how the girls deserved a better quality of employer. Things got hot between me and this guy, and we both knew it was going to be a fight, but before I could touch him, he reached under his fur coat and pulled out a gleaming black revolver that seemed unusually enormous. He smacked me across the face with it, and I fell to the ground, dazed and inebriated, but I saw him point it in my face through my blurry vision. Then he drew back the hammer with his thumb.

The pimp made the best decision for all of us. He grabbed the rifle and ran. By the time we were in a taxi, I had the makings of a spectacular black eye, which we all felt was a fitting reward for a fantastic night out.

Chapter 13: Setting the Tone

By the time Telemachus Clay aired, the work on the Harlem site was coming to an end. Thankfully, my eye had returned to normal by then, much to Stanley, the bartender's chagrin, who felt it made me appear dangerous and seductive. Anne, on the other hand, was not a fan of the black eye or the narrative, and she was sick of my drinking. I don't blame her; I was getting tired of it, too, but what could I do? I was convinced that if I didn't drink, I'd be locked up in a psych facility. Anne, being a Highland girl, never tried to encourage me to stop drinking. She wasn't a stranger to whiskey, and she snorted just as much coke as I did, which, in true cokehead terms, wasn't much. We were more like drunks.

Following that, we all headed to the groovy Pyramid Club on Avenue A to watch the trannys dance on the bar and listen to a new band named They Might Be Giants, who were onstage in the back room. Everyone complimented my performance in the play, even if they didn't understand why a midwestern farm lad parading around a pretentious improvised set supposed to portray Hollywood's debaucheries would talk with a Scottish accent. I explained that it was because my character was a child, but they didn't seem to comprehend it. To be completely honest, neither did I.

Steven and I struck up a conversation, and I liked him. He'd come to New York on a Fulbright grant, which he informed me was significant for a painter. He was ready to have his first solo show at the Barbara Toll Gallery and asked if I would come along since it would be wonderful to have someone with my kind of midwestern accent around. I said I'd be overjoyed.

Steven called me on the day of his opening and asked me to meet him in a Bowery pub. He stressed how essential it was and how frightened he was. I had just gotten home from work and was still wearing my overalls, so I stepped into a cab.

We were very toasted by the time we got to his opening, and the entire New York art scene was already there, fawning over the gigantic paintings Steven had painted. He finished one a week while commuting to and from his studio in Bed-Stuy, Brooklyn, and his SoHo penthouse Monday through Friday. He took the train every day and ate the sandwich his wife made for him for lunch. He was a really kind man.

Then Roswell started smacking, and I had no patience for that scene, so things went quiet for a bit. Then Chad Moran arrived in town.

I hadn't met Chad when we were both in Glasgow, but I'd heard good things about him. He was renowned as a dangerous and unpredictable maniac as well as an electric musician and an incredible front man for his band. He wasn't violent in any way, but he was known for climbing up buildings, jumping out of automobiles, and streaking whenever the mood struck him. He also went missing from time to time. When he went missing, a scheduled televised appearance in London had to be cancelled, only for him to reappear a few days later in the confined ward of a psychiatric hospital in Aberdeen, 600 miles away. A drunken binge, a little amphetamine sulphate, and a lack of sleep had sent him into a momentary insanity, and he had been apprehended by police as he "shot" imagined monsters with a toy gun in Aberdeen's railway station, much to the chagrin of respectable passengers. I could identify with Chad. I have been that insane on occasion. If I had been smart enough to hallucinate a weapon, I would have shot the murderous ducks of Kelvingrove Park.

His band had done well, selling some CDs and filling several large theatres, but the record label finally became tired of Chad's antics. That kind of behaviour is only tolerated if you are producing a lot of money for these cretins.

Chad told me that this rum tasted so wonderful to him that he felt he had been Captain Morgan in a past life--his surname was Moran, after all--and proposed that we drink it till we passed out and chatted like pirates all day. That sounded like a good strategy to me, so that's exactly what we did.

Chad was fearless in his quest of a good time, which I found infectious, if not captivating. I wanted to be near him. He made me appear to be the rational one. I didn't know it until years later that Chad wasn't much crazier than me, just a few stations ahead of me on a train that was going nowhere.

Chad and I were inseparable for a spell, partying and carousing all over town. I became the drummer in his new band, The Tonesters, and despite never playing a single gig, rehearsing, or even being alone in a room with musical instruments, we had a few meetings at record company offices in Manhattan based on Chad's U.K. reputation. My other buddies despised him. Steven the artist had no time for such nonsense; he was far too serious and downcast. Roswell believed he was more frightening than the IRA people from uptown, and Jamesy thought he was just another New York morality tale waiting to happen.

I recognized she was correct, that it was the prudent thing to do. In New York, everything appeared to be spiralling dangerously out of hand. My tourist visa had expired years ago, and it would only take one arrest to have me deported and never allowed to return, and anyone with half a brain could see--even I could see--that an arrest was unavoidable. So, after a little more than a year in the East Village, Anne and I gave up our belongings, said our goodbyes to our friends, and returned to the old country.

I spent the following three or four years, like many people who come to New York to live and then have to leave before they really want to, with the vague impression that there was a wonderful party going on somewhere and I wasn't at it.

Chapter 14: The Gong Show

We both agreed that returning to Glasgow would save our relationship, but we were wrong. The move exacerbated our difficulties and, if anything, expedited the demise of our marriage, though I'm not sure it could be considered a marriage in any other sense given my selfishness at the time.

I not only got my job back at the Chip Bar, but I also got promoted. They assigned me the title of "chargehand," which meant that in addition to bartending, I had to manage the other employees and balance the cash register at the end of the night. Surprisingly, working hard in the company of that much alcohol was not a difficulty for me. I enjoyed being in charge, and because the bar was constantly loud and full, I rarely had time to stop and have a drink myself. It wasn't something you could do when inebriated, and it was simply too focused. Of course, I drank some beers while working, assuming that if I appeared like I was having a good time, the customers would, too.

I approached the job as if it were a show, smiling and joking with the clients and attempting to create a friendly and pleasant environment for those who came there to forget about their own nonsense for a bit. More than anything else, bartending taught me how to be a stand-up comedian.

I worked long hours, sixty or seventy per week, and Anne and I only saw each other periodically in the filthy single room we had rented from a spiteful divorced landlady who shared the building with her big collection of incontinent and grumpy cats.

Michael observed me working the bar for a time before asking if I had ever been a performer. I told him about Telemachus Clay, which made him laugh, and I also admitted that I had tried an open-mike spot at the Comic Strip comedy club in New York but had had minimal, if not terrible, success. My audience of intoxicated mafiosi didn't understand my accent but still despised me.

Michael was intrigued by my narrative and shared an idea with me. The Tron Theatre had a big public bar with a raised platform at one end, which Michael planned to turn into a stage every Friday night where amateurs could try their luck in a "gong show." He believed I should do it after seeing my shenanigans behind the bar and learning about my interest in the performing arts.

It took me several weeks to come up with an act. I chose to mock all the uber-patriotic native folk singers who seemed to infect every public performance in Scotland and who appeared on local television every New Year in the yearly orgy of maudlin, folksy sentimentality known as Hogmanay. Despite the fact that everyone I knew believed these men were the worst, I had never seen anyone openly go after them. Attacking anything homegrown may be considered unpatriotic, but I was willing to take the chance, so I made a little song about how sexually attractive sheep are and prepared a short spiel. I pulled together a costume out of my wedding suit, which had been shrunk beyond recognition by an inept dry cleaner, and a terrible green sweater I had received as a Christmas present from a relative who had to despise me. I also wore ill-fitting glasses with shattered black frames held together by a Band-Aid and a pair of plastic zip-up Chelsea boots with jeans tucked inside.

I needed a name for my character that would elicit an immediate laugh so that I wouldn't be gonged the moment I spoke. Bing Hitler, the moniker Peter Capaldi had come up with for our little drag performance, sprang to mind. Peter had by that time become a well-known performing actor, and I figured he wouldn't use it again, so I borrowed it. I could have easily phoned him for permission, but that's not who I was at the time.

I finished work early one night, drank a few beers, and went to the theatre without informing anyone, not even Anne. I waited backstage in my garb till the real folk singer ahead of me was gonged off, then Harry called "Next!" and out I walked.

They chuckled at my expression, which was a good indication, but then they grew silent. I approached the microphone.

The audience laughed once more. I'll never forget the strength of the sound. I knew they were with me right away. I continued with my little speech on how Scotland was amazing and everything else was not, exaggerating my point to absurd proportions. Why were Scottish insects superior to English insects, which were effete dandies? Why was the world lucky there were only five million Scots, because if there were more, we'd force everyone to eat fucking haggis, which was better than anything those so-called French or Italian bastards could give. Why being Scottish was preferable to having an orgasm or sex, which never happened at the same time for Bing.

It wasn't much, but it was exactly the kind of inane rubbish that most Scots had been force-fed since we could remember. It was a hit with the audience. When I was done, they yelled for more, but I had none and told them so. They mistook it for a joke. I eventually turned to Harry and yelled, "Gong!" since I didn't know what else to do. He slapped me, but they were still cheering when I returned to the stage.

The audience rightfully awarded the fifty-quid prize to the guy after me, an octogenarian in a tweed cap who performed a furious "Ghost Riders in the Sky" on the harmonica. I, on the other hand, took home a handful of larger awards.

Chapter 15: The Rise of Hitler

Bing was not an instant success. I had nothing to say other than a couple lines of schtick and "The Sheep Song." I booked a few local bar gigs, but I'd die onstage after a few minutes since I didn't have enough material and wasn't yet skilled or secure enough to riff. I made a pitiful appearance at the Cul De Sac pub, which was immediately next door to the Chip and where I was still working full-time as a bartender.

This type of remark rarely endears you to an audience, and this one stormed the stage, seized my instrument, and shattered it in front of me. I dashed out the back door and took a cab that the theatre manager had requested carry me to the nearby train station. As we rushed away, an angry throng pursued us, and someone threw a large rock, shattering the back window and showering me with broken glass. I was quite tipsy and a little worried, but I enjoyed it. In a strange sense, I found it romantic. But I suppose for a nutcase, any attention is good attention. To cover the damages, I gave the cabdriver the price I received for the gig (always obtain the money up ahead).

Victor and Barry, for example, were a comic couple who wore dressing gowns and sang campy and hilarious ditties about aristocratic Scottishness. I wasn't wild about them (perhaps because I was jealous), but the majority of folks loved it. Victor and Barry were played by two young actors just starting out in their careers: Forbes Masson, who is now a very prominent and recognized actor in Scotland, and Alan Cumming, who you may recognize as one of Broadway's leading women. Lynn, too, was part of a comedic double act. She and a fellow student established the Alexander Sisters, a humorous parody of desperate middle-class Scottish matrons, after attending the Royal Scottish Academy of Music and Drama.

Sayle. I told myself that being in comedy was nearly cooler than being in music, yet whereas London was packed with comedy clubs, Scotland had none. The majority of my performances were as openers for rock bands or at nightclubs, where they expected me to amuse drunken hipsters who were immediately irritated that the music had been turned off for me. In these circumstances, the heckling began before I even got to the microphone, forcing me to adopt an especially confrontational demeanour. Sometimes I won them over, and sometimes I irritated them. My rage, combined with too much booze, often made for a miserable evening for everyone.

A drunken heckler approached the stage one night while I was performing at the Rock Garden--the bar where I met Peter Capaldi and joined the Dreamboys years before--to take issue with me over a joke in my act that he didn't like. I proceeded to embarrass him, but he was too intoxicated to sit down and shut up, so he lunged at me, and I, being a drunk Glaswegian first and a comedian second, knocked him out cold, necessitating an ambulance for him and a hasty escape for me out the kitchen door, escaping his pals and the cops.

These tapes were aired on a late-night alt-rock show and received a positive response, despite the fact that the act sounded dry--just a person in a studio talking in a funny voice. That form of comedy requires real people in front of you, or so I believe. I'm more energised, and I enjoy the rapid reaction that a live audience provides. Nonetheless, I was spreading my name, or at least Bing's name, to more people who appeared content to watch me live. When the DJ stopped the music to announce to me, the nightclub guests genuinely cheered.

I quit my work and applied for unemployment benefits, establishing myself as a legitimate member of the entertainment industry.

We had finally obtained a mortgage and were living in our own modest ground-floor apartment on Maryhill Road. It was a cheap, shabby, contemporary structure on a major street that I despised. I found it difficult to be around Anne, who was always angry--with reason, I may add--because most evenings I was arriving home too late and too intoxicated. Some nights, nothing. Anne showed up with several of her pals at a grungy after-hours party in someone else's place, while I was sitting on the living room floor talking to a very lovely female. I had no idea she'd be there, despite the fact that we lived in the same house and were apparently a relationship. We were both quite inebriated, and Anne quickly informed me that I had disrespected her one too many times, and while I have to admit she would have been correct on a thousand other occasions, I was really just talking to the lady in this case. Anne, on the other hand, was a Highland lass, full of fine whiskey, mad as hell, and refusing to take it any longer. She took off one of her stiletto heels and began bashing me over the head with it, producing a magnificent commotion and a large amount of blood.

I left the party with the lovely girl after drunkenly telling her our marriage was gone, which I don't think surprised anyone. We visited her home.

Later, Anne and I attempted to mend things; she was remorseful, as was I, and there was true affection between us, but it was impossible. She was a generous person who desired a life, marriage, and children, while I was a selfish asshole who desired beer, sex, drugs, escape, and adventure, and I blamed her for our departure from New York. We were completely and utterly incompatible.

Anne got me an inflatable atlas globe for my birthday that year, along with a greeting card that said, "I give you the world."

Have a good time blowing it up.

Chapter 16: On the Train

My life was changed by the Edinburgh Festival in 1986. I haven't worked a regular job since. Because of my TV appearances, I was able to perform at larger venues in Scotland. John McCalman, the man who got me on local radio for the first time, proposed we record a comedy album for the small record label he ran. I jumped at the opportunity. I taped Bing HitlerLive at the Tron Theatre over two nights. It became a cult hit, which indicates that many people heard and enjoyed it. However, no one seemed to profit from it. Definitely not me.

I wasn't aware that my career was progressing at the time, and I wasn't even aware that I had a profession, but I see now that things were going swiftly, despite my limitations as a legitimate human being offstage.

Our aim was to put on a live show featuring music and comedic performances interwoven with sketches, similar to the concept of Saturday Night Live. Making live television is challenging enough in the best of conditions, but when you're in Scotland on New Year's Eve, it becomes even more difficult.

This was due to the network's change of heart over their "edgy" and "hip" position after rumblings in the Scottish press that this new show would dishonour the tradition of Hogmanay.

I've seen it a million times in the show industry. In the television, film, and music industries, executives begin with a bold idea, but as the moment of truth approaches, they lose their courage and return to what they know.

Scott and I butted heads, just like we did when we were youngsters. He wanted me to do what he said, and I told him to fuck off. We didn't talk for a bit after that, but not for long. There was alcohol to be had, and we both root for the same pitiful football team, Partick Thistle. Within six months, we were back to our old ways.

The New Year's Eve show was a dreadful experience, but it had its highlights. During rehearsals, Jimmy Mulville and I became friends; we would sit in his hotel room for hours, doing lines of coke, drinking beer, and chatting nonsense. Sandy McDougal, an eager, tubby, and fairly gauche network executive, decided to join us one unforgettable night. He claimed to have "done tons of coke" during his "extensive world travelling," but Jimmy and I were sceptical since when it was his turn to snort a line off the mirror with a rolled-up banknote, he exhaled instead of inhaling, blowing the valuable white powder all over the carpet. Even today, when I run into Jimmy, who has been clean and sober for a million years and is about as far away from that world as anyone can be, he looks irritated at Sandy for this. I am as well.

But I wasn't making much money, so I'd travel the 400 miles from Glasgow to London by "luxury" coach, "luxury" meaning the vehicle had a small bathroom in the back. It was a dreadfully uncomfortable journey, similar to travelling a Greyhound bus, except slower and damper, and once there, I'd crash on Peter Capaldi's couch.

Peter and I had remained close since the Dreamboys, and he had now moved to a little cottage near Kensal Green Cemetery in Northwest London, just a short distance from the horrific Dennis Nilsen serial killings. The bizarre, scary atmosphere suited him perfectly, and we spent some freezing-cold winter days together, wearing enormous black jackets and smoking cigarettes as we walked around the ridiculously overdone Victorian tombs of that colossal graveyard. Withnail and I had our own little period. Peter was always nice and helpful to me, and I punished him by taking advantage of our friendship and showing up unannounced to his house, leaving a horrific mess in my drunken wake. I thought we were fine since I could make him laugh, so I was surprised when he told me that until

I treated him and his life with a little more respect, I was no longer welcome. Years later, I eventually had the decency to apologise to him, which he accepted with his customary compassion and elegance. Peter is without a doubt one of the most outstanding and impressive people I've had the pleasure of knowing.

Harry was accompanied by two of his friends, Paul Whitehouse and Charlie Higson. Charlie was the singer for the indie rock band the Higsons. I'd heard them, and they were really decent, but Charlie had no interest in music, so he went into writing, which was his true passion. He created science fiction stories as well as jokes for Harry. Charlie was a reserved person at first, but after he got to know you, he transformed into a gregarious and funny friend in arms.

We left London early one July morning, Harry, Paul, Charlie, and me, along with Rachel Swann, the Truly Scrumptious of London agents, and a few entertainment journalists and managers. It seemed like a field trip.

Long before it became an institution, the Montreal festival was in its infancy. Nobody has even heard of it. For the British comedy world, we were the canaries in the coal mine. We had a great day canoeing on the St. Lawrence River's rapids and hanging out with the festival's crew of gorgeous, young French-Canadian females, not to mention the outgoing and entertaining American comics.

I became friends with Rick Siegel, a New York City talent manager who, at six-five and two-forty, was one of the biggest people I'd ever encountered. San Francisco comedian Steve Kravitz refers to him as "the mutant Jew."

He told me that the neighbourhood was changing beyond recognition because property developers had moved in and all the old characters, as well as the majority of street crime, were leaving. That wasn't such a bad thing, he added, but it seemed to come with a significant loss.

Jamesy mentioned that something was dying. It just didn't feel the same. And he was correct: it was not.

He also explained why I couldn't find my old actor buddy Roswell, the person who advised me to attend my first acting audition and who was my doorman companion at Save the Robots.

Ros had died.

He had fallen in love with heroin more than it had fallen in love with him. I was astounded beyond words; he was the first of my pals to perish. I went uptown to O'Tooles, but no one I knew was there. It was all manicured hedge-fund pricks in those multi coloured collared shirts.

I went to the Last Resort Bar in search of my old theatre pals. The pub was vacant, and half of the patrons and staff had left. The AIDS epidemic was wreaking havoc on the world. In fact, it seemed to devour and dominate the entire city of New York. In that community in the late 1980s, everyone was talking about their HIV tests or how scared they were of developing or already having AIDS. I was afraid and depressed by the time I boarded the plane to go. I've never been happier to leave New York City, before or since. As the smelly old train rumbled out of Central Station and across the Jamaica Street Bridge, I peered out at the orange halogen street lamps reflected in the black water of the Clyde. I looked around at the deteriorating Victorian structures that will soon be sandblasted and refurbished into yuppie hutches. I watched the revellers and rascals make their way through the gleaming wet streets. I reflected on the excitement and risk of my childhood, as well as the anxiety and frustration of my adult life thus far. I reflected on my marriage's demise and my own failures as a man. All of this was visible to me through my reflection in the dark window. I went down the tracks, oblivious to the fact that I was getting further south with each passing second.

Chapter 17: Jimmy's Wedding

My friendship with Helen was my first indication that love could be the answer. At the very least, it was enough to keep the more visible signs of my alcoholism at bay for a while.

We met on the set of a TV show that Jimmy Mulville, who was now working both in front of and behind the camera, had hired me for.

Chelmsford 123 was the name of the sitcom. Set during the Roman Empire's occupation of Britain, it was a little high-concept, but still quite entertaining. Helen had been hired as an ancient British hag, while I was to portray a Roman actor disguised as a Scottish savage. The role required her to wear a hideous wig with (fake) dead mice in it and to have parts of her teeth blacked out. Although I thought she was hilarious and intriguing when we talked at the craft services table, I can't say I conquered my aesthetic fascism and fell in love with her right away. But that wouldn't take long.

There was a party for the cast and crew after the episode we were filming concluded, and she came over to talk to me. It took me a few seconds to realise who this stunning woman was. I'd never seen her without her costume before.

Soon after, Harry and I went on tour again, roistering around the smaller theatres and student unions of England and Wales, so Helen and I didn't see each other for a time, but I called her frequently from the road and we talked for hours. I learned everything I could about her.

In a nutshell, she was out of my league.

The tour Harry and I were on was set for a two-week run during the 1987 Edinburgh Festival, where we'd be performing at the Assembly Room, a far more prestigious location than I had been the previous year. Helen came in wearing a flamingo-coloured summer dress one day when I was drinking in the Artists Bar, a hangout for the performers and their guests. I saw her standing at the doorway, backlit by the cold Edinburgh sun, and I literally lost my capacity to breathe for a second. I summoned her over as soon as I recovered, and while we hugged a little too long for a cordial greeting, it wasn't long enough for me. I could have spent the entire day there.

I hadn't bothered learning to drive, and riding public transportation in full Highland regalia-kilt, sporran, sgian dubh (the ceremonial knife worn with the kilt)would have been awkward, so I took a taxi from my tiny rented North London flat to Chelsea.

Denise had requested me to wear the full rig, so I agreed. She and Jimmy had been very gracious to me, even allowing me to stay in their spare room until I could find a place of my own. If she wanted the whole Brigadoon, that seemed like the least I could do.

I'm not sure how much fun the bride and groom had at their wedding, but Helen and I had a great time. We danced and danced and danced, and she didn't seem to notice when I went off to the restrooms to do coke lines with the boys. Of course, I drank and drank and drank, but the coke, along with the dancing, kept me looking sober enough to be able to leave with Helen at the end of that fantastic evening.

I've heard ladies complain about having to take the "ride of shame" the next morning, when they have to take the metro home in what they wore the night before and everyone knows what they've been up to. I understand exactly what they mean. I didn't have enough money (coke is pricey) to take a taxi home from Helen's the next day, so I had to cross London on the underground, very conspicuously.

For the first time in my life, I was hungover, ashamed, trembling, and deeply in love.

Chapter 18: The Aspirations of a Phoney Englishman

I don't know how to explain Helen and me. How do you define love? We were just there for a short time. She wanted me to move in with her soon after the wedding, and I did, though I retained the modest flat across town for the first several months in case she kicked me out.

We were together for five years, and at the end, she had changed my life beyond recognition, with my permission. I had asked her to, and I was and continue to be delighted and appreciative that she did.

She insisted on me learning to drive and getting a licence as well as a car. She informed me right away that she didn't want a lush for a lover. So I didn't get drunk for a long time when I was around her, which was rather often because we lived together.

She altered my eating habits, introducing me to fresh fruit and, saints preserve us, muesli. We slept at night and woke up in the morning--a mind-boggling thought for someone who hadn't lived like this since his freshman year of high school. We went to the movies, the theatre, and dinners with pals we hadn't met in bars! We even went on vacation to Seychelles, Barcelona, Sri Lanka, and France. In short, Helen was an adult, and in order to be with her, I had to attempt to be one as well. She showed me how to live while being the sexiest and funniest person I'd ever met. She also smelled wonderful.

In London, the only people I knew were the newlyweds Jimmy and Den, but Helen knew everyone. Her acting pals were comfortable and easy to get along with, but when we went out to dinner with her older (and, in fact, closer) friends, I had a dreadful sense of inadequacy.

They were Oxford and Cambridge graduates who "came up to

London" after graduation and tended to keep together. Helen Fielding, Richard Curtis, Douglas Adams, Hugh Laurie, Stephen Fry, Rowan Atkinson, Emma Thompson, Angus Deaton (Helen's ex--I distrusted him till I saw him), and Geoffrey Perkins were among Helen's gang of ineffably creative beings. All of these people were highly prominent in British comedy, and I felt quite uneasy around them, feeling that they looked down on me because I didn't go to a fancy school or come from the "right" family, but I now realise that was nonsense. If somebody was unreasonably prejudiced toward me, it was because of my history. I didn't want anyone's fucking assistance or influence. I was superior to them because, I don't know, I was Scottish, angry, or whatever. Also, I didn't know how to act in the presence of these smart individuals who treated me with tact, charm, and sympathy, not because they scared me, as I persuaded myself at the time, but because they loved Helen and knew she loved me.

I stayed intoxicated for a week while filming a Channel Four documentary at the Pamplona bull-running event in Spain. One night, I struck up a conversation with four American film crew members who were in town filming second-unit footage for a Billy Crystal picture called City Slickers. When I told them I wanted to go to Hollywood and work in the film industry, they laughed. They said they already had enough jerks like me.

I visited the United Kingdom once more with Harry Enfield, but this time it wasn't as a double bill.

Harry had become a tremendous success as "Loadsamoney," the persona he and Paul had created--a vulgar nouveau riche London plasterer. On this trip, Harry received the most attention, Paul and Charlie were secondary characters in his skits, and I was the opening act.

I was grateful for the work, but also bitter and resentful, despite the fact that Harry, Paul, and Charlie were all gentlemen who never gave me reason to feel that way. I was just feeling that way.

When I came for an eleven a.m. appointment one Monday, I was worried since Peter Cook has always been a comedy god to me and countless others. The thought of meeting and possibly working with him was almost unbearable, but I managed to ring the doorbell intercom, and after a brief period, a very recognizable, although slightly tired, voice responded.

We had breakfast when Peter came downstairs in an extremely short terry cloth robe. He was a kind and outgoing man, very generous about comedy and his own life, and a hilarious and enlightening conversationalist.

We talked briefly about the project, and then blabbed on for hours about the comedy scene, both past and present. He was aware of the Bing Hitler nonsense and knew a lot of the individuals I was working with. He was interested in comics in general and was always up to date on who was doing what. We talked about my life a little bit and a lot more about his, which was intriguing. He spoke glowingly about his former co-star, Dudley Moore, who went on to have a tremendous cinematic career in America with Ten and the Arthur films. He plainly adored Dudley, but felt that his success in America had not fulfilled him.

Nobody can live a double life indefinitely, and mine was coming apart at the seams. My love for Helen, or, more precisely, the force it wielded against the swelling tide of my drinking, was starting to fade.

I rarely got drunk in front of Helen in our early years together, but if one of us was out of town, I'd pour liquor down my throat like a man possessed, which I suppose I was.

But now I was getting drunk all the time. It wasn't that I didn't care; I just couldn't stop myself. I was out of control, and whenever I needed to make a good impression at a party, dinner, or performance--I'd get so bombed that I messed it up.

I was pulled over for a DUI one night while driving from the Groucho to Heathrow Airport to pick up Helen. She'd been working in Africa for the British Comic Relief Charity and had returned home fatigued, having to find out what had occurred (though she knew by this point it would be reasonable to presume I'd gotten drunk and screwed up) and get herself and her stuff home.

Meanwhile, I was in jail, and her automobile had been seized. (For a change, my own rusty old bus was in the shop.)

I'm still curious what Helen got out of it all. What made her put up with me? I believe she knew I loved her as much as I was capable of loving anyone at the time. And, for some reason, she adored me. Thankfully, she had the foresight not to marry me.

We had done everything we could to establish a life together. We bought the most charming property in Dunwich, a tiny Suffolk village whose population increased from twenty-three to twenty-five when we moved in, as soon as I was making enough money to persuade the bank to offer us a mortgage. We hid from everything in the bleak beauty of the East Anglian coast. We decorated the home and got a washing machine and a refrigerator, I chopped firewood in the garden, Helen made jam, and it was heaven for a while. Then, eventually, everything came crumbling down.

I left for London early one Monday morning to conduct some business. Helen sent me off to the train station; it was a two-hour train ride, and I promised her I'd be back about four o'clock.

I arrived in time for whatever nonsense meeting I had planned and then proceeded to the Groucho. I drank a beer with someone, which led to another beer, which led to a coke line with someone, which led to a talk with a girl. As a result, I didn't get home until Thursday. I was too preoccupied with tearing about London with my cokehead pals, passed out on people's floors or hotel rooms. I know it's ridiculous, and I'm not sure how to explain it, but this is what occurs when I drink alcohol.

When I traversed the long country paths back to the house in Dunwich three days later, I felt like a very sorry soldier. I was expecting wrath and nasty ultimatums from Helen, but instead found her packing her bags--in fact, most of her belongings were already gone--and was extremely sad. We entered the small kitchen with a view of the North Sea. She sat in my lap and made me some tea. We gripped each other as fiercely as we could. We cried and cried and cried some more. I'd never fallen apart like that before in my life, and it was hard for her as well, but when she had enough breath, she told me what we both knew was coming.

I went for a walk on the lonely Walberswick marshes outside the village after she had left. I did something out there that I hadn't done since I was a farty small schoolboy in the wretched damp town church. I said a prayer. I begged the God I still don't fully comprehend and have difficulty believing in to assist me--either kill me or change me.

I'd turned into someone I detested, and I couldn't break free from whatever spell had been put on me. I was incarcerated in a prison I built myself. I assured Him I would go to any extent to get out.

I'm not sure if my prayers were answered because I'm not an Evangelical or even a particularly religious person.

However, things picked up speed after that.

Chapter 19: The End of Daze

After a few days alone in the vast empty country house, snuggled inside a whiskey bottle, it dawned to me that because I was no longer with Helen, I could return to America. Helen would never have left Britain--she loved it there--and I would have followed her wherever she went, but it was all over now.

It was time to go to the States. A new beginning.

Unfortunately, I was broke and couldn't make the journey without at least some cash. Borrowing cash from the bank was out of the question--I'd already had the last of my credit cards shredded in front of me by an embarrassed liquor-store clerk who had contacted Amex to find out why I'd been rejected.

I got a few gigs and made some money, but I couldn't keep it up because, with Helen gone, the brakes were off and I was constantly getting fucked up, which wasn't cheap.

Finally, I got a break when the BBC placed me in The Bogie Man, a film set to be shot in Glasgow. It stars Robbie Coltrane (Hagrid in the Harry Potter films) as a lunatic who believes he is Humphrey Bogart and ends up solving a real crime. Fiona Fullerton, the lovely English actress who played a Bond girl in A View to a Kill--she takes a Jacuzzi with Roger Moore and is slain while wearing a sexy scuba outfit--was cast as an investigative journalist who had an affair with my character, a detective. I had no idea why they chose me, unless it was because all Glasgow officers are inebriated. Actually, now that I think about it, I understand why they chose me.

Fiona and I went out for dinner after the first day of rehearsal, got drunk, and ended up in bed together, beginning an affair that captivated the British tabloid press. Nobody knew what this lovely famous English rose was up to with the little-known, overweight, inebriated vaudevillian. I couldn't figure it out either. Fiona is a sweet, bright lady who should have known better. I imagine she fell for whatever nonsense I was spewing at the time, and she hoped, like many women who found themselves with men like me at the time, that she could transform me, that whatever good she saw in me could be nourished with affection, sex, and home cooking. But I was far too damaged for that. I was far out at sea.

I returned to London when the film was completed, practically destitute. I still had the modest property in Dunwich, but I couldn't bring myself to visit it; it was a tomb for an old dream. I spent the money I made on the movie before I earned it.

I spent a lot of time with Fiona in her Chelsea flat, and when I got too wild, I'd sleep on the floor of someone's house or spend the night in one of the rooms available for rent above the Groucho Club.

I arrived at the bar about four p.m. and shared a pint with Tommy, and another with an actor I knew, and one thing led to another blah blah, and I awoke the next morning on a mattress in the storage room above the bar covered in vomit and pee. I hoped it wasn't my own vomit and pee.

I felt the worst I'd ever felt. Worse than the first time I passed out on the sickly sweet Eldorado. Worse than the first stab of chronic alcoholism and panic I felt in Mrs. Henderson's automobile. Worse than fleeing Kelvingrove Park's vicious and partially fictional killer ducks. Worse than I ever expect to feel again.

Worse than before Helen departed.

This time, however, there were no tears. That was the end of it for me.

I was an alcoholic, a loser, and a human disaster. I was nearly thirty, divorced, and bankrupt. I'd lost the one woman I'd ever loved, and I couldn't even make it to Scotland for Christmas with my folks.

The humiliation was terrible. It pressed down on me like a huge weight. And the weight of that burden began to shape a notion as hard and clear as a diamond.

It was time for me to pass away.

There would be no grandstanding; this was a reasoned, reasonable thought, not a plea for assistance. I was about to check out, and that would be the end of it. Farewell, horrible world, and fuck you. Suicide seemed appealing. It felt fantastic. I meant it; this time would be different.

I was both sober and encouraged. I knew exactly what I was going to do: stroll down to Tower Bridge and swan dive into the dark, filthy Thames. The river would carry me out to sea, together with all of London's waste. That would demonstrate to them. Despite the fact that I had no idea who they were.

I stood up and shook off my dizziness after making my decision. I scrubbed my face and clothes as best I could at the backroom sink, hoping to look acceptable for the Reaper, before heading downstairs. I could get away from it all without ever having to face Tommy or his family, who lived in the same building as me.

Except for one thing, I hadn't considered. Tommy enjoyed drinking almost as much as I did, and it was Christmas after all.

We each drank long draughts.

God help me, but I can still taste how wonderful that sherry tasted as it went down. Bitter and sweet, rough and silky, all at once. As if the Lord himself had lifted his cool hand to my furrowed brow, the heavenly tonic eased the palpitations of my irregular and agitated heart and restored my breath from shallow panic to even serenity. I entirely forgot about killing myself as the warmth of a thousand loving suns flowed through me.

And I'm not even a fan of sherry.

I, like many others before me, found redemption in alcohol and Jesus.

People who have never had a morning drink have no concept how soothing it can be for alcoholics.

It actually saved my life.

Chapter 20: Rehab

Jimmy Mulville has always thrown me little pieces of work despite my drinking and failures, all of the bad performances and no-shows. As he grew in power as a producer, he'd get me a part in a sitcom here or a stand-up gig there, even though we no longer socialised. I'd never seen him out and about and had heard reports that he'd been in treatment.

Jimmy threw me another bone in 1991, when he offered me a position on his hugely successful Saturday-night panel show Have I Got News for You. I rewarded him by being awful. The show consisted of a few smug guys talking smart about the week's news stories, and I was too shy to speak. I later spotted Jimmy in the green room. I felt the tales had to be real because he seemed all sparkling and religious or something, but I didn't dare to inquire. He saved me the hassle by telling me. He said he'd gone to the country to sober up, and for some reason, I felt terrible for him. I ran as fast as I could away from him because he terrified me.

Meanwhile, I continued to deteriorate. Fiona and I joined the other intoxicated revellers in Parliament Square in London on New Year's Eve 1991 to witness the hands of Big Ben chime at midnight. As the audience counted down the final seconds of the year, I felt a breeze and looked at Fiona.

Jimmy utilised his newfound clout in the alcoholic rehab industry to secure me a spot at Farm Place, one of the top addiction rehab institutions in the United Kingdom, if not the world. It was prohibitively expensive, and I couldn't afford it because my personal debt, including the money owed on the Dunwich house, approached a quarter-million dollars, and I didn't have health insurance, but Farm Place put me on credit, which they rarely do. Jimmy apparently put in a word and informed them that if I made it, I wouldn't be able to live with myself if I didn't repay them. That I'd rather die than owe anyone money for their assistance.

Jimmy apparently understood more about me than I did about myself at the time.

On the cold and dull morning of February 18th, 1992, my younger sister, Lynn, poured me a glass of warm white wine. Lynn had subsequently moved to London and lived near the flat I'd once occupied with Helen. The wine was to calm my anxiety before I attempted the cure. Jimmy arrived at nine a.m. in his huge, toasty, expensive automobile.

That was the end of my drinking. On a Tuesday morning, a tepid liebfraumilch.

Kirsty informed me that there were both male and female patients here being treated for various addictions such as alcohol, drugs, sex, food, gambling, and so on. Meals were served at specified times each day, and no one was allowed to skip them. (I assume this was more for the benefit of the anorexics than for the alkies, since we almost rarely skip a meal). Every weekday, two-hour group and individual therapy sessions were held in the morning and another in the afternoon. Later, I would be assigned a counsellor. For the first ten days, no visitors or phone calls were permitted. Every patient slept on the premises and shared a room with at least one other person. There will be no fraternizing (as in fucking) with the other patients. And no medications at all.

Patients were expected to assist with maintenance chores, and anyone who the counsellors felt was endangering the health or treatment of other patients or disrespecting the staff might and presumably would be asked to leave. I assured her I understood, and she introduced me to Rachel, a nurse. She was another pleasant-looking middle-aged woman with brown eyes, brown hair, and pale skin. She exuded the calm and solidity of a protective Labrador.

Rachel led me into her office and extracted some blood. She also took my blood pressure and pulse, as well as prodded my liver and lymph nodes.

"Seen worse," she murmured.

"You're overweight but malnourished." Your blood pressure is elevated, and your liver is enlarged. Your heart is racing a little, but everyone does when they arrive. "When was the last time you drank?"

She nodded when I told her about my glass of wine with my sister. She inquired about my drinking habits over the preceding few weeks.

"Yeah, you're the real deal," she agreed when I told her. "Take these."

She handed me a small plastic container containing a few pills.

"What are they?" I inquired.

"One of them is an anticonvulsant. Guys who drink as much as you do frequently have fits when they quit abruptly. Hemineverin is the other. It's a modest trance that will keep you from going into delirium tremens. "Have you gotten them yet?"

I had lived in terror of the rumoured terrible visions that afflict habitual drinkers but had not yet struck me. I told her the same thing.

"Lucky. I'd guess it's a few days away. That's how many alkies die. DTs caused heart failure.

Hallucinations simply frighten the poor bastards to death."

I informed her that I did not want to use drugs. That I had not come here to do drugs.

"Listen," she continued politely, "up until now, I would say that ninety-nine percent of all the narcotics you've taken in your life were purchased from guys you didn't know, in bathrooms or on street corners, or something like that." Correct?"

I agreed by nodding.

"Well, these guys could have sold you salt or strychnine." They didn't give a damn. They wanted your money. I'm not interested in your money, and, unlike your past suppliers, I went to college to learn about the best drugs to offer to individuals like you to help you get better. So, with all of that in mind...take the pills!"

I used the medications.

Later, I sat alone in the TV room, waiting for the other patients to finish therapy. The heminevrin was making my nose itch like hell. I switched on the TV but kept the volume very low so as not to disturb anyone. There was a Gillette razor commercial on the air, with lots of square-jawed guys playing sports and hugging their dads, kids, or wives, all with the healthy sheen and perfect teeth I associate with Americans. The advertisement jingle trilled cheerfully, "Gillette-the best a man can get."

I fixed my gaze on the television. What has become of me? I was supposed to be one of those guys, active, athletic, successful, and, most importantly, American. I planned to walk on the moon, become a movie star, a rock god, or a comedian. I was going to live a wonderful life with Helen and die like Chaplin a thousand years later in my Beverly Hills mansion, surrounded by my beloved family and the sorrowful world media. Instead, I was simply another mediocrity in show business. A drunk who puked in his pants and fled for rescue.

My life had been reckless and self-centred. My single thought, my sole objective, was pleasure in the moment. I had disappointed and wounded anyone who had been foolish enough to love me.

I was far from being the finest a man could be.

Chapter 21: Reboot

Brian, my rehab counsellor, stated that I had been suffering from an illness, that alcoholism was not merely an indication of a morally inept mentality, but an inescapable malady for those who were afflicted. It was a line I'd heard before, and I dismissed it as a lame explanation for my behaviour. Brian, a mega-tanned, mega-handsome ski instructor type who looked unnervingly similar to the dudes in the Gillette commercial, said he didn't care what I thought or how I felt; whether I or anyone else accepted the concept of alcoholism as a disease didn't matter; what mattered was that those who suffered from it were most likely to recover when treated as a disease. So, why argue about it?

I have to admit, that made sense. Brian also promised that I would not be absolved from making restitution to everyone I had wronged. To get and stay sober, I would have to clean up the debris of my past. The notion was intimidating, but also consoling, because the counsellors insisted it could be done, and many of them were recovered alcoholics themselves.

Let's call them Matthew and Lucerne, my roommates. Matthew, a sixty-year-old Church of England clergyman, was receiving treatment for the first time. After one of his parishioners approached him about a drunk he'd observed sleeping on top of the tombs in the churchyard, Matthew felt he needed to get aid before anyone found it out.

When Jimmy arrived to get me up two months later, I was "clean and sober and didn't care who knew it," in the words of Raymond Chandler." My self-assurance didn't last long; it was already fading on the way back into London. We passed what seemed like a million pubs, and I felt extremely exposed. How was I supposed to avoid bars after spending my entire childhood in them? Jimmy predicted that I'd figure it out.

I believe it is the only option for me to keep my right to be sober.

I remained with Jimmy in London for a few nights before returning to Glasgow because I had a job there. Philip Differ, a BBC producer who'd previously worked on a Bing Hitler special, had offered me a series of my own. It would only be broadcast on BBC Scotland, not throughout the United Kingdom, but it was a tremendous offer that Philip didn't turn down even when he found out I was in Show-Business Hospital; he simply delayed the start of production until I was released. As a well-known TV producer, Philip had met many alcoholics, but I believe I was the first he knew who had sobered up, and it thrilled him. When the suits threatened to cancel the production due to my experiences in recovery, Philip supported me, and we went on to co-create a couple other programs. Philip's warmth and unwavering dedication were enormously helpful in putting my life back together.

The good news was that I'd be spending the first few months of my recovery in Glasgow, where I'd be less likely to slide back into old habits. By this point, I hadn't lived in the city in five years and had forgotten where the cool pubs were. Thank you, God.

I met John Naismith, a Scottish businessman and former alcoholic who lived in London and who would become a type of guardian angel to me, through Jimmy.

He grew up just outside of Glasgow and had lived a life quite similar to mine, except he was fifteen years older, both chronologically and in terms of quitting drinking. John had shown enormous promise as a young guy, but his alcoholism was always dragging him down. He agreed to help me along the path to something like normalcy because he had stopped drinking long before I did. Given the striking similarities in our origins and life stories, it seemed like a natural fit. John would keep an eye on me and help me get through those first few difficult months of abstinence, while I would serve as a reminder of what it was like to be insane and how dumb it would be to try drinking again. What began as one ex-drunk assisting another grew into a deep and valued mutual connection that continues to this day.

Some people, I suppose, regain their sanity the moment they get sober. That was not the case for me. I believe I became even more weird after rehab, but I was just a little better at disguising it than others. My head was rumbling like a slum. Being alone there felt hazardous, especially at night. I had nightmares virtually every time I closed my eyes, making sleep impossible, and for a while I experienced terrifying bouts of wrath that I had difficulty comprehending, let alone regulating.

I was still looking back over my life--where I'd fallen down, where I'd tripped, where I'd taken decisions that were, at best, rash. John guided me through this difficult time without ever making me feel judged. As I described a tough or embarrassing episode from my history, he would often bring up one of his own that matched or even surpassed mine in some manner. It was difficult not to be impressed by how insane he had become. My moods became more balanced. I was less terrified and far less angry.

I was ready to start going through the process of making amends, contacting numerous people I knew I'd wronged, telling them I was sorry and that if there was any way to make things right, I would. I didn't call the following people: John advised me that the best way to make amends with them was to never disturb them again. But my ex-wife was not among them.

The most difficult decision I had to make, and the one I dreaded the most, was contacting Anne. I just felt so bad about how I'd treated her that I didn't know where I'd get the courage to call her and couldn't imagine how she'd react. In the end, fate forced my hand. One day when I was walking home from the BBC, I turned a corner and there she was. I inquired whether she had time for coffee, and she answered yes. We went to a neighbouring café, and I told her how I felt about being such a jerk, and how desperately I wanted to make it up to her, to make things right between us. She burst into tears. Then she told me she was glad I had found a better way to live and that she didn't think I was entirely to blame for our marriage's failure--a startling thought that I had not considered in my self-obsession. Anne claimed that she had been so consumed by her desire to settle down and start a family that she couldn't or wouldn't recognize how insane I was, how incapable of giving her what she desired. She still loved me, and the only way for me to make peace with her was to be happy.

I have a knack for spotting beautiful women.

On the way back, I told him about the time he took me to that record store and how much it had affected me, and how he got the bus driver to stop at Moodiesburn so I could have a wee boy poo in the old lady's magical lavatory.

Of course, he had no recall of it, but he made sure we stopped for restroom breaks on the way home.

Chapter 22: Buying a Knife

After six months of sobriety, I started to feel a little better. I was in great physical form because I worked out every day; I was more confident, happier, and, to be honest, horny. My employment in Glasgow ended, and I didn't feel like I belonged there, but I was too young to attempt America, so I returned to London.

I'm not sure what happened to London during my six-month absence, but something had changed. It didn't appear as dark and dismal, nor as frightening or threatening. And, by George, the gals were lovely. My sobriety made a huge difference in that town.

While hunting for an apartment, I stayed in my friend John's spare room for a few nights.

I didn't have much money to spend on housing because I was still paying off debts. Though I had pondered declaring bankruptcy, John informed me that I would have to repay everyone, with interest. I'd been sober for seven years by the time I paid off all my debts.

I located an attic flat in central London near Regent's Park, close off St. John's Wood High Street. I met two more expat Scots, Philip McGrade and Alan Darby, through John. For various reasons, neither of them drank, but they knew how to have a good time and set about teaching me that talent.

We formed a little Caledonian mafia, a wee Scotia Nostra, with John. These individuals are like brothers to me and remain my closest pals to this day. Philip, who eventually immigrated to America, currently works as a writer on The Late Late Show with my sister Lynn.

We'd gather in coffee shops and restaurants in London, see movies, bands, and comedians, and, most importantly, chase females. They didn't run too rapidly.

English girls, particularly those in London, are sociable, sassy, confident, humorous, and fun, and they want to have a good time. They also tend to favour boys with Scottish accents who aren't completely intoxicated. Chelsea's friendly women brightened my first two years of recovery, and I will be eternally grateful.

The first lady I met in London was a striking redhead who worked during the day as a counsellor in a treatment centre and at night as a drummer in a band called the Lower Companions. She approached me at a party and told me to call her Rock and Roll Susie, which I gladly did. She was older than me and a lot of fun, a woman who sucked the life out of you. Susie was well aware that I was new to sobriety and not a smart long-term bet. This was great with her because she didn't want a real relationship in the first place. I think it's a win-win situation.

I was hired to play a little part in a BBC-TV Christmas special called One Foot in the Grave while dating Susie. They took me out to southern Portugal for two weeks to film it. I was overjoyed to acquire the position, not only because I desperately needed it, but also because it reconnected me with Peter Cook, whom I hadn't seen in a long time. Because our filming schedules were a little different, I arrived before him, shot a scene, and then took a few days off before returning to the set. Susie flew out from London during the interval, and I met her at the airport in the tattered and stinky Renault 5.

I paused for a while to consider this. Then, much to the chagrin of the Portuguese commuters, I made an illegal U-turn and drove east across the Portuguese border into Spain. We drove down the southern coast on hot, dusty, desolate roads bordered with orange and cork trees until we arrived in Algeciras, a shabby port town. We took the auto ferry over the Straits of Gibraltar that night, the Renault stowed in the hold. There was no wind, the sea was smooth and peaceful, and a low crescent moon hovered above the Atlas Mountains' dark silhouette. As we approached the Moroccan shore, I could hear the call to prayer emanating from the minarets, indicating the end of the day's devotion.

Susie bought some beads and dangly earrings, and I bought a big curly scimitar with imitation gems embedded on the ornate handle the next morning while we went around Tangier. We drank mint tea with a Bedouin tribesman who tried to sell me whatever he thought I would want--a carpet, hashish--before getting back in the car and driving back to Portugal in time for me to get back to work. We completed the unusual and lovely journey in three days. It occurred to me that if I had continued to drink, I would have lain by the hotel pool the entire time, getting smashed. I felt like I was finally getting the hang of being sober. I was in a wonderful mood.

Peter Cook arrived just as Susie landed back in London, and he appeared as delighted to see me as I was to see him. We went out for supper after the day's filming, just the two of us. I didn't bring up my lack of drinking, and if Peter noticed, he didn't say anything, despite the fact that he gladly drank wine throughout dinner. While we were enjoying dessert, some of the other actors and crew people walked in and started an impromptu party. After that, we all went to a nearby nightclub and danced to horrible house music for two hours before heading to the beach to smoke our wacky tabacky and drink our duty-free brandies. Before everyone went back to their hotel rooms, it was daybreak, and several of us had hooked up with people we shouldn't have.

Later that day, after finishing recording my role, I was collecting my belongings to return to London when I heard a tap at the door. It was Peter, who appeared solemn and uneasy. I'd never seen him quite like this before.

"Can I talk to you for a minute?" he inquired.

"Of course," I answered as I led him in. "What is it?"

He said he'd been following me the night before in the restaurant, the nightclub, and on the beach and hadn't seen me take a sip of wine or a hit from a joint. I assured him he was correct and that I had not.

"Yet you seemed to have a great time."

"I did," I admitted, my cheeks flaming at the prospect of having to confront Susie when I returned to London.

Peter paused for a time before asking, "How do you do that?" in a softer voice than I had ever heard him use.

I told him it would take some getting used to, but that if he wanted, I could introduce him to some individuals in London who could assist him. He replied he did and promised to phone me when he returned to town.

I hadn't heard from him in months, but then he called and said he was almost ready to get sober. He grabbed me just as I was about to walk out the door with my luggage packed to begin a two-month tour of the United Kingdom as Oscar Madison in The Odd Couple. I gave him a few phone numbers and said we'd hook up when I got back.

Before it could happen, Peter died. His body finally succumbed to the continual barrage of booze. I still wish I could have done more to aid him.

Chapter 23: The Aspirations of a Phony Frenchman

Rick decided to organise a little party around the time of the Oscars. His management company was thriving: I had completed a pilot that may turn into a series, and he represented several others in the same situation. Rick believed that this was the appropriate time for his clients and friends.He thought that his affordable condo in West L.A. would become synonymous with Hollywood's up-and-comers. He couldn't afford to have the party catered, so he enlisted the services of a girl he met in New York and her roommate to help pour drinks and serve the pizza that had been delivered.

It was a Saturday afternoon event hosted the day before the Oscars, and it was already in full gear when I arrived. I've felt very weird at gatherings since I got sober--as opposed to my drinking days, when I was great but everyone else felt awkward--and have developed the habit of going straight to the kitchen if one is accessible. In my experience, the most intriguing people always end up there, and there's very little risk of you being dragged onto a dance floor.

I spoke with Rick for a while, and he introduced me to a couple of his other clients, including a grumpy actress who subsequently went on to star in a TV sitcom and an opinionated Scientologist. Rick informed her that I was foreign, and she was completely taken aback. "Where are you from, France?" she inquired, her nasal twang irritating.

"Oui," I answered, and because she didn't stop talking, I claimed I couldn't understand her so she'd leave me alone.

Just then, the girl from New York who was assisting Rick walked in, wearing a striped Shirt that clung closely to her magnificent breasts and a pair of trousers with so many novelty patches that there seemed to be little actual denim left. The patch that drew my attention was spherical and crimson, with the words "Sex Has No Calories" written in white characters on it. She inquired whether I was from Europe after hearing me dismiss the actress in French.

"Oui," I said once again.

She rambled on in French that I had no hope of understanding. But it didn't bother me. I enjoyed staring at her wide brown eyes and her gleaming American teeth, and I was content to be thus close to her breasts. I merely grinned and nodded when she finished speaking.

"You have no idea what I just said, do you?"

"Not a word," I said.

Then she grinned her beautiful smile, and we got down to business.

That is how I met Sascha.

We took one of those little cable cars that rise halfway to the stars on a vacation to San Francisco. It was a clear day, unusual for that city, and I'm not sure what triggered the idea; perhaps it was the blue of the sky, the romance of the tram, or the sweet breeze coming off the bay. Maybe it was the view of the legendary island jail Alcatraz, but I asked Sascha to marry me before I realised what I was doing.

She looked surprised, then said, "What you mean is that you're happy and wish you could feel like this forever."

"Yes! Exactly!" I gratefully agreed.

We dropped the subject, but it would come back to haunt us.

My house-sitting gig on Amalfi Drive came to an end just as I learned that Maybe This Time had been picked up for a series. ABC ordered thirteen episodes, and I rented a cool bachelor pad on Sunset Plaza Drive, where the rich(ish) trash of Los Angeles congregates every lunchtime to watch each other pick at overpriced chicken salads, the men in Armani and aftershave and hair dye, and the women in silicone and leopard skin. I really wanted to be a part of all that sleazy splendour, but Sascha wouldn't let me, and she despised my new place right once. I was only there for six months until Sascha and I moved in together, renting a small house in Laurel Canyon. The Scottish Daily Record back home stated in its gossip column that I had become engaged to an American woman named Laurel Canyon, in a usual display of breathtaking error. The item had a purported "insider's" evaluation: "Craig and Laurel are very happy, said a source close to the couple."

I was content with Sascha at the time, at least at home, but work was a pain in the a$$. Perhaps This Time was killing me. I was horrified by the writing, as much as I enjoyed working with Marie and Betty and the other key actors, Amy Hill and Dane Cook. I just couldn't keep my mouth shut about how bad it was, or stop giving suggestions to fix it. None of this endears me to the writing or producing team, but where I come from, an actor is treated as a collaborating artist rather than a hired gun, so I approached the task in a way that is far from typical in American television production. I eventually chose to leave after much deliberation with Sascha. I'd made enough TV rubbish in the UK and didn't want to repeat myself in America. Before I officially quit, I told Betty about my decision, and she felt it was gutsy, if a little rash. Marie was taken aback. Some Mormons even showed up at my trailer to attempt to talk me out of it. I thanked them for their suggestions and waited silently, knowing they'd felt uneasy enough to depart. They were very wonderful individuals. It's not easy to break out of a TV deal just because you don't like the writing. I'd need approval from the studio's head, the Dark One, the Earl of Hell himself, Dean Valentine.

I still believe he's kinder than he lets on.

The cold, brutal reality of unemployment follows the joy of quitting. I continued to write and rewrite my screenplay. While the tale wasn't particularly to her taste, she enjoyed my writing enough to recommend me to another producer who was searching for a writer to collaborate with him on a project.

Mark Crowdy had discovered a local news article in his home county of Cornwall, England, about a respectable woman who had been convicted of growing marijuana in her greenhouse to avoid financial issues. He assumed it was a TV show. I mentioned that it sounded more like a movie. That pleased him.

After a pleasant lunch at Café Med on Sunset, the amiable and engaging Mr. Crowdy requested me to work on the script with him. There was no money in it just now, but if the picture was done, I'd get paid and maybe even cast.

I didn't have anything else planned, so I accepted, and we began work on a film called Saving Grace.

Chapter 24: The Fat Man, the Gay Man, Vampires, and Marriage

Mark and I worked Monday through Friday for roughly six weeks and finished the first draft. Then he proceeded to London to begin the lengthy and difficult work of gathering funds for production. He believed that because the film was set in the United Kingdom, he would have a greater chance of having it funded there, which made sense to me, but in the meantime, I was left with nothing to do. Sascha and I went on some travels, and because we were running out of money, I changed my "no auditions' ' policy and auditioned for everybody who would look at me, but I didn't get a bite. For nearly a year, the only paid job I got was a one-episode guest stint as the ex boyfriend of the show's star, Nancy Travis, on the struggling sitcom Almost Perfect.

We were soon living off of Sascha's savings and money borrowed from Rick. During this difficult and stressful time, I finally decided to quit smoking, which I found far more difficult than quitting drinking. When you stop drinking, you lose weight and start to feel better, but when you stop smoking, the reverse happens, at least at first. I think I was a touch argumentative, because after I'd calmed down, Sascha told me that she'd had her stuff packed and in her car for three days.

I met another British writer, the prodigiously creative Sacha Gervasi, through a friend of a friend, whose sense of humour reminded me of Peter Cook. He, like myself, was an ex drummer who had strayed into more literary interests and was now seeking a career in the film industry after obtaining a scholarship to UCLA's screenwriting department. Many people were perplexed when he and I became great friends because he had the same name as my girlfriend, though I never got the two of them mixed up. For the sake of clarity, I will now refer to him as Gervasi, although this should not be interpreted as a sign of hostility on my behalf.

Gervasi and I were talking about my previous life in Glasgow one day. I told him about my gay roommate Robbie, who he felt was hilarious and interesting enough that Gervasi suggested we produce a movie script based on him. Again, because I had nothing but time on my hands, I accepted on the condition that if we ever made the movie, I'd play Robbie. So I started another time-consuming project that wasn't helping me pay my rent.

We renamed Robbie Crawford Mackenzie, made him a hairdresser instead of a waiter, and wrote up a story about Crawford travelling to Los Angeles in search of fame and money. It was a hairdressing sports story, or, as we put it, "Rocky in curlers."

Even while it was fun to write funny screenplays on spec with my pals, I was making nothing, we had spent all of Sascha's funds on rent and car bills, and the generous Rick Siegel's generosity was wearing thin--he wasn't making much himself. I was running out of options. That's probably why I agreed to audition for the role of the Hispanic photographer in Suddenly Susan, a sitcom pilot produced by Warner Brothers Television for NBC and starring Brooke Shields.

Rick brought the script to my house so I could prepare for the audition, and I read the dialogue that I was expected to speak with dismay. I practised my Latino accent on Sascha, who looked like she was about to burst with laughter. I tried once more with my friend John, who happened to be in town on one of his numerous business travels to California. John agreed with Sascha that my accent was pathetic.

"But..." he said, "you should go audition anyway." What else are you supposed to do but sit around and complain? Furthermore, you never know what will turn up."

Sometimes you can't argue with John. So, despite knowing I was in for great humiliation and ridicule, I hopped in the rattly old white Bronco and made the low-speed chase to the Warner lot audition.

I was correct about how it would play out. The entire situation was really unpleasant, and I couldn't believe the producers had even allowed me to read for the job. I've since learnt that casting directors may occasionally purposefully include people who are absolutely inappropriate for a job in the audition process in order to make their other options appear better. It's perverse, but it's a common procedure.

I avoided the strange eyes of the other performers, all of whom were actual Latinos waiting outside the room with me. When it was my turn, I ran through the sequence a few times with an intern reading Brooke Shields' lines. The producers were amazed as I tried hard to seem Hispanic, openly giggling at my Speedy Gonzales-meets-Braveheart accent. On the second pass, I decided to play along, hamming it up and being wildly over the top on purpose, which I believe alleviated some of everyone's humiliation. They thanked me for coming, and as I was leaving, a cheerful-looking, dark-haired man stood up from the desk next to the puzzled producers and approached me.

"My name is Tony Sepulveda. I work as a casting director at Warner Brothers Television."

"Well, thanks for seeing me today, Tony," I responded, preferring not to chastise him for dragging me into a scenario in which I clearly had no chance. There was no point in being a jerk about it now that it was over.

"Do you, by any chance, have an English accent?" the man asked.

"I think I just did," I confessed. "Although I was trying to sound Mexican."

He grinned and told me that, while I was clearly not the appropriate fit for the job of the Hispanic photographer, they were now casting for the second season of The Drew Carey Show and wanted someone to play Drew's snotty English boss. Was I fascinated despite the fact that it was only for three episodes?

I stated that I was.

There was a quick meeting with Bruce Helford, the show's producer and co-creator--a Tolkienesque character who was little, dark, and bustling, like some kind of superintelligent alien hamster from a more sophisticated world than our own.

The meeting was a formality--the character wouldn't be on the air long enough to require a lot of attention--and when Bruce asked if I could do an English accent, I replied in my best Latino, "Sí, señor." I was all in.

That's how I ended up portraying an Englishman on American television for eight years rather than three. My first episode went well; the cast and crew were comfortable and pleasant, and after a week, the producers asked Rick if I wanted to join the cast full-time. He almost cried, either because he was overcome with joy for me or because he knew I would finally be able to repay all of the money I owed him.

My life was transformed by The Drew Carey Show. Not only did it allow me to repay Rick, but it also allowed me to begin lowering my debts from the United Kingdom. I was seven years sober before I was able to pay off everything I owed--over $250,000 plus interest. It was a hefty bar bill. During my vacation from Drew following my first season, I landed a role in The Revenant, a groovy comedy vampire film. (It was released on video under the title Modern Vampires.) I had a great time camping it up with corn syrup blood and busty actresses playing victims.

Although Mark Crowdy had yet to raise the funds for Saving Grace, he had gone perilously close several times. For a time, it appeared like the film would be filmed, especially after Oscar contender Brenda Blethyn indicated interest in playing the lead. However, another screenplay I co-wrote with Gervasi about the hairdresser version of Robbie, titled Je m'appelle Crawford!, performed much better. It created a bidding battle, and the eventual winner, Warner Brothers Films, decided to cast me in the lead. After my second season of Drew, we shot it in and around Los Angeles, and it was eventually published as The Big Tease because Warner felt Americans wouldn't go to see a movie with French terms in the title. I'm not joking.

We shot a scenario where my character checks into a shabby motel on Sunset Boulevard one day. While waiting for the director to call "action," I overheard one of the cops on the radio remark, "Okay, we've shut down Sunset, you guys can go ahead and shoot."

It amazed me that I had only been in America for a little over two years and had already managed to block Sunset Boulevard, if only for a few minutes. I was overjoyed with myself.

I was earning enough money for Sascha and me to leave our rented cottage and purchase an old Spanish house in the Hollywood Hills. We even rescued two dogs from outside a coffee shop, and while the dogs were free, Trump would have been terrified by the vet fees.

It was a domestic paradise for me, but Sascha was unhappy with us living together without being married. I wasn't sure if that was a good idea, but I really liked her. I was also a little afraid of her, and I despised confrontation, so I consented to marry her.

Sascha's Jewish New York family drank hard with the Scottish throng into the early hours of the morning at the wedding, which was held in a large downtown Los Angeles hotel. Drew and my other castmates, as well as the show's producers, were present. It was a wild occasion, with the two cultures mingling on the dance floor in a riot of yarmulkes and kilts. Everyone had a good time, but be warned: the Jewish tradition of dancing the hora with the bride and groom hoisted high on chairs is liable to clash spectacularly with the Scottish tradition of wearing kilts with no underwear, so be prepared for fainting relatives.

Chapter 25: Success and Failure

Saving Grace was shot in Cornwall during Drew's third break in 1999, due to Mark Crowdy's Herculean fund-raising efforts. I played the pothead gardener beside the incredible Brenda Blethyn, who just by being in a film makes it better.

If you've read this far, you've probably deduced that I'm a grump, but perhaps "ungrateful wretch" is a better description. The word "driven" is sometimes used to characterise me, but I believe it is also wrong. I hardly ever let myself be driven somewhere. I am a rambunctious alcoholic/control freak.

I despised the work but adored the money.

I used to be a hooker.

In some ways, I felt like I was breaking the agreement I had made with the cosmos in the Mojave Desert.

I was meant to pick between safety and adventure.

I told Sascha about my frustrations, and he continued pushing me to quit, but I didn't have the guts. We went into serious financial difficulties the previous time I quit a job, and I didn't want to go through that again, though I suppose that was simply an excuse. Things were growing heated between Sascha and me, but I was hesitant to confront him.

I was gone all the time, filming or attempting to set up movies, and I should have made her my partner and taken her with me, but I didn't, so she found something to be excited about on her own. She became involved in Pilates, which was then the new physical fitness craze sweeping L.A. She utilised part of our funds to create a studio in the heart of West Hollywood, complete with all of the bizarre mediaeval-looking Pilates equipment. When I told her I didn't want to marry a CEO because I'd never see her again, she answered I never saw her anyhow, so what was the difference--and she had me there.

I'm not sure what I said, but according to Sascha, I just laughed like a fool and refused to let her ride her bike home.

We had just recently decided to try for a kid, and it happened so quickly that I believe we were both taken aback; thrilled, but taken aback. That's probably why you've been given nine months to get used to the concept.

Saving Grace was released while Sascha was still pregnant. Fine Line Studios gave us premieres in both New York and Los Angeles. It was the first picture I'd ever worked on that had good advance hype and ended up being a hit; it even won the audience award at Sundance. When it happens, a slew of strangers begin kissing your a$$. The dishonesty is frightening. I had to be careful who I listened to, so I chose Sascha.

I sat silently in the back of an absurdly enormous vehicle with my wife on the way to the L.A. premiere at the Egyptian Theatre.

"You taking this in?" she inquired.

"What?" I inquired.

"You're attending the big premiere of a film you wrote and starred in." This is why you came here--anything else will just be variations on this."

But she was mistaken. I adored Saving Grace and am still proud of it, so I wanted to publicise it and see it prosper. I was about to discover how uncommon that is in the coming years.

Sascha's forecasts, on the other hand, can be frighteningly correct. For example, we were leaving David Letterman's New York studio following my first-ever appearance on his show to promote Saving Grace.

"You're going to be asked to take over for him one day," she told me.

I told her she was crazy since I was an actor and writer, not a late-night television host.

"I'm telling you," she said emphatically.

As I write this, no one has even proposed that I take over for David Letterman when he retires, but I think it's a little more likely than it was when I first saw the program, and I'm certainly more interested in the concept now than I was then. We'll see what happens.

Our first encounter was in the rooftop suite of the Istanbul Hilton, and I don't think I'd ever been so terrified about seeing someone in my life, given that this person had been a world-famous rock star-the rock star-for as long as I'd been alive.

Fortunately, Mick was used to people being anxious and stumbling about him, and his easy chuckle and generous attitude quickly put me at ease. He picked up the phone to order us lunch--I could hear the room-service operator's eager yelling across the room--and as we waited for it to arrive, he informed me about his idea.

To keep me pleased, Mick's producing partner, Paramount Studios, offered me a three-picture development agreement.

Of course, I accepted the job and spent a lot of time on the phone with Mick over the next six months, but no matter how hard I tried, I couldn't turn the story into a movie Mick wanted to make, even if Paramount was pleased with the script.

Mick continued asking whether it could be "more edgy," until I finally exclaimed, "Mick, what exactly do you mean by 'edgy'?"

He went on to say, "Well, you know that film As Good As It Gets, with Jack Nicholson?"

"Yes," I said.

"Well, could it be more like that?"

I told Victoria I had no idea what Mick was talking about. She looked compassionate at first, then dismissed me a week after I turned in the second draft.

Chapter 26: Crash

I developed a spec script called The Family Business with Philip McGrade, a long time buddy since we first met in London when I was freshly sober. It's about a has-been rock star who discovers he has a daughter he never knew about. It was a horrible story, but ultimately uplifting, so when I pitched it around the studios, there was some interest. We eventually struck a deal with Morgan Creek Films, who agreed to let me direct the film as well as star in it. I assumed that as director rather than producer, I would have more control over the film's destiny, but I was greatly misled, especially with Morgan Creek participating.

It's an independent studio owned and controlled by James "Jim" G. Robinson, a Baltimore businessman who had a distribution deal with Warner Brothers at the time. You'll recall that Warner botched my last film, but that's showbiz; you can't hold a grudge for too long or you'll never get anything else created. Jim is a forceful, brash man who likes things done his way, and I am as well, so our relationship was challenging. Jim is a good businessman, but he's no filmmaker, and he has the taste of a carny with a head cold. However, if you want Morgan Creek to direct your film, you should not inform him.

I was overridden, but the casting of Charlotte, who isn't all that horrible in the film, might not have been so disastrous if Morgan Creek's "development executives" hadn't spit all over my script. Changing the music, the lines, and the title of the film from The Family Business to the repulsive and vapid I'll Be There. Basically, it was basically sweetening the whole thing to the point where it became an expensive Hallmark Hall of Fame movie.

As much as I'd like to blame those guys, it was entirely my responsibility. I should have been stronger from the start, saying "Fuck it, no way!" and abandoning the endeavor. Because I was eager and desperate to make my first film, I caved and wrecked it.

Never, ever again. I'll never fuck again.

I discovered that making a movie you are not proud of is just as difficult as making one you love. To top it all off, I was in a motorcycle accident halfway through production, which meant I had to act and direct with a fractured collarbone and three shattered ribs. In addition, it was summer in the United Kingdom, which exacerbated my hay fever, and every time I sneezed, a white-hot bolt of pain raced through my ravaged skeletal frame.

Sascha and Milo came to visit, but I was in such bad company that my wife whisked our son to Paris with her friends.

I finished the film, which opened to a resounding disaster in the United Kingdom in May 2003. Warner refused to release it in the United States, so it went directly to video. I'd spent a year of my life on a movie that had destroyed my marriage, devastated my career as a filmmaker, and been absolutely no pleasure at all. Even after taxes, commissions, and travel, I didn't make much money.

I also attended the Cannes Film Festival in May 2003, expecting to raise funds for another film and save the doomed I'll Be There, but I returned away extremely discouraged and empty-handed.

It was time to do some spring cleaning. I felt that no one had shielded me from the calamity, that the agents had been slackers, and that Rick, my friend and manager for the past eight years, had been outfoxed. I dismissed everyone, and I hoped I could have fired myself as well. I stopped in Paris on my way back from Cannes. As I went about the city, trying to figure out what to do next, I felt like I had hit a brick wall. I decided that if I ever had another narrative to tell, I would do it as a book rather than a film, so I wouldn't have to work with a bunch of people I wouldn't trust with a fork.

As it turned out, I did have a tale idea. It was about a Scotsman who has many obstacles but eventually prevails, albeit in a rather cryptic way.

It would take the form of a novel, and even though I had no idea how it would end, I would begin writing as an act of faith.

I went back to my hotel and scrawled on a piece of embossed Georges Cinq notepaper, "Fraser had a problem." He had the difficulty of wanting people who didn't know him to like him."

With that sentence, I began to construct a bridge to a new freedom. I'd discovered a media that didn't require any participation or consent. Other than the PC I already had, I had no equipment. There were no union rules and no producers. I was free to do whatever the heck I wanted.

After all this time, I discovered that the novel is punk rock.

Every day, I raced to that book like it was a bottle of whiskey and dived inside because it was a universe over which I had at least some influence, and it gradually began to take shape over time.

Chapter 27: Latecomer

A late-night talk-show host should be cool. I am not implying that I am cool in the least. I'm a middle-aged white man with greying hair, a cinched waist, and a frightening laugh. That is not acceptable.

I'm not claiming to be a late-night talk-show host any more than I am a stand-up comedian, writer, actor, drummer, or milk delivery person. Late nights are all I do anymore; it's my work. The job itself is interesting.

If you're a late-night talk-show host, a little bit of cool goes a long way. Consider the competition: if Dave wasn't the late-night king, he'd just be a grouchy old man who drives too fast. Jay would be a strangely needy mechanic, and Conan would have youngsters calling him names as he walked down the street. Jimmy Fallon is a thirty-five-year-old giggly adolescent without his show; and Jimmy Kimmel is a lovely person, but he'd be the first to acknowledge he's not cool--in another life, he'd be a charming maître d'.

When I agreed to guest-host The Late Late Show, I treated it like an acting audition. I did some study on the character I'd be portraying, on people who actually did what I'd be claiming to do.

If Dave was the greatest of the current crop, which I feel he is, I wanted to know who he thought was the gold standard and how they worked. I'd read that he respected Regis Philbin as a broadcaster and revered Johnny Carson, so I went through a ton of old Tonight Show tapes and watched Live with Regis and Kelly every morning.

Dave was correct. Johnny was fantastic; you adored him. Regis was amazing in a different manner, like he was your closest friend, uncle, and father all rolled into one. Here was a TV Proust, a man who could turn the most banal moment of his life into five, occasionally 10 minutes of interesting discussion. I spent hours studying these three guys, Dave, Johnny, and Regis, not to emulate them, but to pick up a few suggestions. I'm not sure what I learnt, but I had a lot of fun.

I arrived the night before my scheduled slot at CBS Television City in Los Angeles to get a feel for the location and, of course, to see what type of act I'd have to follow. Damien Fahey, the night's guest presenter, was a young man, so I stood in the green room and watched him work. He appeared to be competent enough to take over permanently. Michael Naidus, the segment producer who had shepherded my guest appearances on the show while Kilborn was the presenter, reached me. Michael is a pleasant individual, so I felt at ease conversing with him. He asked whether I was excited to give it a try the next night, and I answered of course.

But I was incorrect, and Peter was correct, and thus began a pattern that continues to this day on The Late Late Show. He is still the show's executive producer, and practically every day I am wrong and he is correct.

Back in the green room at five o'clock the next afternoon, I heard the show's announcer, Richard Malmos, call my name, and I walked out onto the floor of small Studio 56 to revel in the raucous acclaim of a paying audience who had no idea who I was.

In any case, I enjoyed it.

For a brief while, you are Johnny. I'm convinced that's why we all do it, Dave and Jay and Conan and the Jimmys and me, because you get to feel like Johnny every now and then.

I also felt at ease in front of a television camera--eight years on The Drew Carey Show had vaccinated me against any ugly adrenaline rushes. I recited the gags from cue cards, but the writers had collaborated to construct Kilborn's TV accent and had about as much in common with me as I do with Dakota Fanning.

The material was generic and mostly lame, but after seeing Johnny on tape and how he handled bad jokes, I was convinced that somewhere in there, fucking around between written gags--the glue between inanities--lay the key to me landing the job I so desperately desired about five seconds into my first night as guest host.

I evidently yakked it up with the visitors in a satisfactory manner, which I didn't find difficult at all. I was genuinely interested in what they had to say, and Brenda Blethyn had given me an essential acting lesson on the set of Saving Grace.

Approximately fifty people had guest-hosted the show, some of them very huge stars doing it for pleasure, and some of them very big stars who wished to appear to be doing it for fun lest they be picked.

The competition was eventually reduced to four candidates. They were: D. L. Hughley, the lineup's only genuine name; Damien Fahey, the boy who had gone on the night before I did; Michael Ian Black, the popular trendy comedian; and myself.

We'd each receive a week of shows to demonstrate our abilities, and then Worldwide Pants and CBS would choose one of us. I was confident that D.L. had nailed it because he was both experienced and amusing. Dave was said to prefer Damien Fahey, which was proven when Damien came as a guest on Letterman during the auditions. I was worried about this until I watched the broadcast and realised that if Dave was hot for this guy before they started talking, he rapidly cooled off.

I didn't see what the other guys did because it would have been like watching someone else kiss your girlfriend, which was horrible enough, and then watching them do it better than you, which was even worse.

During the major late-night bake-off, I was fortunate enough to secure a guest position on Life As We Know It, a floundering ABC show starring Kelly Osbourne. I was to play another rock star, Kelly's character's father (where do they get their ideas?), and while I wasn't thrilled with the screenplay, they were filming in Vancouver, which would get me out of L.A. and away from all the speculation about who would win The Late Late Show. I also hoped that the task might occupy me enough to alleviate some of my agitation.

I drove my car from Los Angeles to Vancouver; a road trip is always a good distraction for me, and at the time, I would only fly if absolutely necessary.

Michael Ian Black was up last, and when he ended his Friday-night program, I called the other Michael (Naidus-The Late Late program producer). Mr. Naidus had by then become my insider; he told me everything he knew, and although he didn't say it, I could tell he was cheering for me. He stated that CBS President Les Moonves would hold a conference call with David Letterman, Rob Burnett, and Peter Lassally the following Monday morning, and that the final decision would be taken at that time. These were the four horsemen I had to be concerned about that weekend.

Speculation about who it would be was rife. I had a gut feeling Peter was on my side. We had just clicked the moment we met. Others were a different story.

I, like the other three contenders, had met with Les Moonves, and I believed it went well. Anyone who has dealt with Les would tell you that he is a straight shooter. He'll shoot you, but it'll be straight; he comes across as a guy who is simply too busy for nonsense, and I admired him for it. I looked him in the eyes and assured him I wanted the job and would not let him down if he gave it to me. He nodded.

"I know you wouldn't," he said, but he didn't reveal his choice.

I knew I wasn't Rob Burnett's first choice, and what Dave was thinking was anyone's guess, though he subsequently admitted he didn't pay much attention to the whole thing, leaving the selection to the others.

The anxiety was overwhelming. My work was over in Vancouver, so I bit the bullet and flew to New York, where my girlfriend, Andi, was visiting relatives. I was depressed and felt that I was in for a big disappointment. Andi may have thought I was miserable company since she recommended we go see something on Broadway to take my mind off things.

After that, we went to Joe Allen's for supper with Brenda. Andi and I kept the conversation focused on how much we appreciated her performance while remaining diplomatic about the content.

There was still no news on Monday morning, which I interpreted as bad news. I flew back to Vancouver, planned to spend the night there, have dinner with some friends, and then drive back to Los Angeles to lick my wounds.

When Peter Lassally and Rob Burnett called, I had just checked into my hotel room.

"It's you," Peter said.

Then I did something unexpected.

I hung up the phone, knelt, and murmured, "Thank You."

Chapter 28: Riding the Pass

Peter invited me back to Los Angeles the next evening for dinner with him and Bill Carter, a New York Times reporter who had published a best-selling book on Jay and Dave's late-night spat. Bill had agreed to write a story for the Times about my takeover if he could meet with me, and since he happened to be in L.A. at the time, he couldn't say no. On other matters, Peter thought this was a fantastic chance that I should not pass up. I told him I wasn't going to.

The only problem was that it was already noon in Vancouver, and I needed to get my car back to L.A., which meant driving all day, sleeping in a motel for a few hours, and driving all day again the next day if I wanted to make the dinner date. I didn't dare to leave my car in Canada and fly because I was still shaken and nervous from the bumpy six-hour flight from New York that morning, and I was convinced that the gods of irony would kill me in a terrible plane crash just after I had scored the biggest professional coup of my life. Within fifteen minutes, I was in my car and driving out of the hotel parking lot.

My phone began to ring almost immediately. The CBS press department was the first to schedule interviews for me on the long drive south. I spoke with radio stations, local newspaper journalists, magazine writers, and TV critics, and we all agreed on one thing. We couldn't believe I got the job. That's when I started to get a smell of the common belief among them all: that I'd fail. Even many who admired me were uncertain that someone with an accent would be accepted as the host of an American late-night talk show. I responded that the current governor of California had an accent so thick that he couldn't pronounce the state's name correctly, so I didn't think people would mind if I rolled a few r's here and there.

I told my family and friends the news in between interviews. I contacted my mother in Scotland, despite the fact that it was late at night; my mother was used to getting late-night calls from me ever since the time in Kelvingrove Park during my last acid trip, when I was stalked by the killer ducks. A few years later, I called her from the Bangkok airport, where I was waiting to change aircraft on my way to Australia. I'd drank excessively on the journey from London and was wandering around the airport when I spotted a Tie Rack store. I bought a yellow tie with little black skulls on it for whatever reason. I had to inform someone since my drunken brain thought buying a tie in Thailand was significant.

"Ma, I just bought a tie...in Thailand. Isn't that amazing?" I said when she answered the phone, I was sleepy.

"That's nice, son, but what will you do with him when you get him home?"

I hung up because I was too inebriated to explain.

This time, however, things were different; I was sober and had actual good news.

"Ma, I just got The Late Late Show. The job I was trying out for."

She was overjoyed for me, however I was surprised when she woke up my father and informed him that I had become a newsreader in America. I let it go and let them sleep again.

I called Business John, my Scottish guru, who told me I was doing well for a hopeless drinker.

Andi, my girlfriend, was overjoyed, but she seemed to know that this was a threat to us.

When I chatted with Sascha, she reminded me of her prediction outside the Letterman studio many years ago.

I didn't have hands-free in my car, and my head was starting to feel roasted from all the driving.

the cell-phone talk. Fortunately, the road began to ascend and curve through mountain passes where reception was impossible. A blizzard was approaching from the northeast, and the weather began to deteriorate. Traffic became increasingly slow.

Night had fallen by the time I arrived at Grants Pass, Oregon. Cars and trucks were creeping down the slick highway, with little visibility.

I eventually arrived at a police barrier, where a cop in a coat with three feet of padding informed me that the pass was too dangerous for cars and had been blocked. He expected it to be open in the morning.

I had nothing else to do, so I turned around and went in search of a cot for the night. I drove to a gigantic Indian casino I'd seen before, but the pleasant, morbidly obese receptionist in bottle-thick specs assured me there was nothing available.

"They had closed the pass," she explained.

"I know," I admitted.

"When they close the pass everything gets full up. There won't be a bed for you for fifty miles."

"I'll die of exposure," I predicted.

"Keno and Blackjack is twenty-four hours long. You can sit in here."

"I need to sleep," I grumbled.

"Well, you're not allowed to park your car in the lot and sleep in it, I can tell you that," she added, winking.

So I trekked back through the snow to my farty potato-chip-and-coffee-smelling car, where I cuddled up in the backseat, wearing two hoodies and two pairs of pants, for my first night as Mr. Bigtime Talkshow Dude.

I felt terrific as I watched the snow fall through the halogen lights in the Four Feathers Casino parking lot. It was ideal. Like the day I discovered I was a billionaire while pulling maggots from my dog's bahookie.

I slept for three hours and then switched on the radio. I drove all day that day, conversing on the phone with additional suspicious reporters, and arrived at the restaurant just as Peter, his wife, Alice, and Bill Carter were finishing their soup. 43

The Beast's Nutrition

It's exciting and fun to guest-host a late-night talk show for a couple of nights. Doing it for a week is still enjoyable, but it is difficult and exhausting. If somebody offers you the opportunity to undertake this job on a permanent basis, I urge you to think long and hard about it since it will change your life--in both good and terrible ways. That forty-four minutes of time you have to occupy between commercials every weeknight just keeps coming at you, day after day.

Then there's the press and some segments of the public that either can't sleep or are interested by late night--again, primarily because of Johnny's legacy and possibly because Dave's enigmatic persona off-screen fascinates them.

The entertainment press believes it their responsibility to haze any late-night newcomer. Conan was panned in the early reviews, as were Jay and Jimmy (both of them), and even Johnny back then. I, too, was not spared. The best explanation I've ever heard is from Bill Carter, who told me, "First they have to forgive you for trying to make them laugh."

That's exactly it. When I first took control, people appeared to be upset. Not dissatisfied or doubtful, but enraged. According to the San Francisco Chronicle, my getting a show proved that the genre was becoming obsolete. Daily Variety despised me, claiming that I provided a helpful reminder to watch Conan. And the New York Post guy said I wasn't only not funny, but also incoherent and appeared to be wearing a wig!

The reviews bothered me. I went on the Internet to see what people were saying, even though I should have known better (and do now). People writing about you under the guise of anonymity can be even more cruel, as they were in my case. I sucked, I should go back to Ireland (!), I was a traitor to Scotland (never quite figured that one out), and someone assumed I was a deviant homosexual because of my accent.

But, for every naysayer, there were sympathisers. The late-night hosts are a fraternity, or at the very least a support group. Jay Leno gave me a pleasant call and wished me luck. Even the great and powerful Dave gave me a welcome telegram. Jimmy Kimmel sent me flowers and a wonderful note that ended, "I hope you know what the fuck you're getting into." That surprised me the most--I had no idea you could still send them.

On my first day at work, my predecessor, Craig Kilborn, also called and was very courteous to me; then Regis Philbin, who turned out to be a great friend of Peter Lassally, took me to lunch. When I say he brought me out to lunch, I mean he ate with me. I paid.

Regis gave me the same advice I received from our mutual friend Peter, Dave, and even Howard Stern: "Be yourself. Make it your own."

They all said that, and they are all giants in their respective areas, but what does "be yourself and make it your own" actually mean in practice?

I was disoriented and out of my element.

Peter Lassally and Michael Naidus were there after every act, as they still are now, with modest advice on how to relax and improve. Advice on how to get through the show without appearing desperate or needy. They progressed from mentors and allies to sincere and treasured friends, with Michael eventually ascending to become the show's lead producer under Peter's supervision as executive producer. I couldn't do the job without them, and I don't want to.

Peter is an immigrant who understands my love for the United States. He is a Holocaust survivor who came to the United States after being freed at the end of the war by Russian Communists, who he claims were almost as terrifying as the Nazis.

I don't complain to Peter about my own childhood troubles. He possesses something that is not commonly seen in the show industry. He is a man who expresses himself plainly and (most of the time) calmly. He keeps his word, he respects people who work for him, and he firmly but respectfully refuses to take crap from me.

"Remember," he said again, "it's after midnight. They don't want you yelling at them. Calm down."

Tips for not scaring children.

"You've got a creepy laugh. Knock it off."

I had no idea I had a frightening laugh, but I'm on the watch now. It appears to be dormant for the time being, but Lassally remains on guard, protecting America's insomniacs from a flare-up of ominous chuckling.

If Peter is unnervingly straightforward, Michael is a natural poker player. By the way I walk into the office, he can know what I'm thinking, and he can shamelessly manipulate me with the classic bait-and-switch and passive-aggressive tactics. He does it on a regular basis in order to get me to do what he wants without a struggle. It's quite brilliant.

"Hey-feel free to say no to this, but..."

With their assistance, I gradually lost the tics that were impeding my progress and weeded out most of the staff members who I thought were not on my side. I used to think I wasn't a competitive person, so I was astonished to hear myself tell the entire team on my first day as host, "This show is number two in its time slot. Anyone who doesn't have a problem with that should quit now."

You must pardon me; I was really ecstatic about landing the big gig and channelling my inner douche bag. For the first few months, I stuck to the standard format of these shows. A few short quips, an overwritten comedic skit, then interviews with two guests, usually plugging their own work, followed by a band or a comic. That had been the format that had worked for years, and I had nothing better. The guest portions appeared to be good, but the comedy was pretty bad, and as Gary Considine, a TV producer who worked on the show for a while, warned me, "Lame comedy will kill ya."

I'm not sure if that's exactly accurate--I'm still doing lousy comedy and the show is doing well. Perhaps it's because it's my lame comedy. I am my lame self, and I own the lame comedy.

Johnny Carson died after a protracted illness just three weeks after I took over. I didn't know how to handle this on air, but Peter stepped in.

"Don't fake anything. Just be honest about what you feel."

So I told the truth, that I only had a few memories of Johnny. I told the audience about my father laughing at The Tonight Show during our first trip to America, and how you had to be incredibly hilarious if you could make a Scottish Protestant laugh. I mentioned my recent binge of viewing all of Johnny Depp's DVDs in an attempt to learn everything I could from the late-night monarch.

We went to commercial after my little eulogy, and Peter came out onto the stage (which is unheard of--he usually watches from a chair in the safety of the control booth) to thank me for what I said about his old friend, and then he exclaimed excitedly, "This is it. Whatever you did just there, that's how you do this show."

I realised what you meant. Just talking off the cuff rather than reading cue cards felt much more natural to me, so over the next few weeks I told fewer and fewer gags and ad libbed more until the writers and I abandoned the traditional method of constructing a monologue--a team of writers composing individual gags, then handing them to a chief who correlates them into sequence. We devised a new technique that entailed all of us discussing for a while and taking notes, then compiling these notes into a list of bullet points that I would try out in front of a live audience on the studio floor. Essentially, the monologue would be outlined but not completed until I performed it on camera. That's still how we do it now, though Ted Mulkerin and Jonathan Morano, the show's lead writers and my most valued creative partners, have polished and streamlined the process.

Some nights it works, and some nights it doesn't, depending on whether I stick to prepared content or improvise practically the entire thing. It all depends on the position of the moon in Aquarius, or my biorhythms, or whatever. I like to think that no matter what night it is, the show is honest.

I tried rebelling against the powerful Lassally's rule by not wearing a tie, which made him very grumpy; but, like a patient parent, he accurately predicted that I would grow out of it.

When I finally started wearing a tie again, it was a black one, which was unfortunate, but it would have been wrong not to.

My father died in January 2006, following a long battle with cancer. I had been prepping performances and flying back to Scotland to see him during his sickness, but when dad died, I was in L.A. I had a gig that night and had no idea what to do, so I called my mother. She instructed me to carry out my father's wishes. My father would have instructed me to go to work.

Remember that my folks express their love through their job.

I knew I couldn't perform a regular show since I didn't have any comedy in me, so we transformed the whole thing into a wake for my father. I rambled on about him, based on some notes I had written earlier in the day. I wanted the guests that night to be mature enough to talk about grief, so we booked Amy Yasbeck--who, sadly, has become an expert on the subject since the unexpected death of her husband, John Ritter--and Dr. Drew Pinsky, because he is not only smart and empathetic but also knows a lot about alcoholics, which meant he'd understand how I was coping. The wonderful Scottish-American group Wicked Tinkers performed as musical guests, and I joined them in raising a little thunder, banging a drum loudly for my father's soul.

I don't recall much about this show and haven't seen the tape, but I heard it went well. He would have liked it, according to my mother. That's all I need.

Dulcius ex asperis is the Latin motto on the Ferguson clan's official crest. It means "sweeter after adversity," and I had the crest and inscription tattooed on my right shoulder in memory of my father, who despised tattoos. The Celtic Paradox is still alive and well in the twenty-first century.

Chapter 29: Settling Down

Andi and I split up not long after I got the show, as she had predicted, and I'd been doggin around Hollywood since then, enjoying my newfound micro-celebrity. I was dating some well-known actresses and getting cited in gossip magazines for dating other well-known actresses I didn't know anything about.

I suppose I was having fun, but this type of activity can grow lonely, and I was afraid of becoming one of those louche old twerps with coloured hair and a brow lift who hang out at the Playboy house. That's what I thought the future held for me until I went to a party in New York City that I didn't want to go to.

Jeffrey Scott Carroll, a wealthy and well-connected Scottish émigré living in Manhattan, had invited me, and I attended because I like Jeffrey. I couldn't get there until it was almost over, and by then I was exhausted and grumpy from an earlier event that I also didn't want to attend, but when you're in New York on a promotional trip, the TV people want to show you around a little.

Jeffrey and I were talking when the most incandescently shimmering woman I'd ever seen came over. When she said hello, he replied, "This is Megan Wallace Cunningham."

I believe I took a step back. Her beautiful blond hair, her sparkling green eyes, her outfit, her earrings, her smile, and, well, everything. I said something along the lines of "Hello, you're lovely, I love you, you have nice hair, let's get married" or something along those lines. I'm not normally anxious around beautiful women, but this one made me completely lose my calm. I probably drooled, spat, twitched, farted, or did something else. Whatever I did made her laugh, and when I saw her laugh, I knew I was in trouble.

Then we started talking. She had no idea what I did for a job, though one of her pals came over at one point and warned, "Be cautious, Megan. He's in the news!"

She used the word "television" as if it meant "serial killer."

Fortunately, Megan didn't notice because she recognized my Scottish accent and her own family was Scottish. She informed me that her grandpa moved from Edinburgh as a young man, dirt poor, and went on to build his fortune in America. She'd travelled to Scotland several times and was familiar with every arcane cultural reference I threw at her.

I was quite impressed.

Nothing occurred that night between us, but we continued in touch over the phone, even though with her in New York and me in L.A., it seemed unlikely we'd ever meet up, just as when I started seeing Helen. I finally persuaded her to come and visit for a weekend after months of long-distance calls. She did, and we fell in love, or, perhaps more precisely, admitted we had fallen in love the moment we met. Then there was a year of bicoastal relationship nonsense, with far too much phone sex and far too many plane miles. Megan finally took the plunge and relocated to my Los Angeles home. Our house, I should say, because we'll be married by the time you read this. I swore I'd never do it again, and I wouldn't have done it for anyone but her, which shows you it's the proper thing to do. Megan is strong, patient, compassionate, caring, hilarious, and knowledgeable about art. She's sexy, clever, and sweet, and I adore her, as does Milo, so we became family. She makes me feel lucky, and I know I am because I have her. I'm delighted to be her husband, and I can absolutely certainly clearly vow that this is without a doubt--and I'm not fooling you--the last one for me. That's fine with Megs.

Chapter 30: American on Purpose

The late-night game has expanded my horizons and taken me in unexpected directions. After years of dormancy, performing a monologue for the camera every night reawakened my ambition to return to stand-up comedy.

I put together some old material and began creating new material before venturing out into the steamy, low-ceilinged comedy clubs to rediscover what I had forgotten. From Birmingham, Alabama, to Bowler, Wisconsin, I moved over the country. Boston to Fort Lauderdale, San Diego to Seattle, and everywhere in between. I resurrected my former trade in front of modest crowds who flock to these tiny establishments every weekend for the chicken fingers and sarcasm. other nights I was good, other nights I wasn't, and some evenings I felt like I was back at the fucking gong show at Glasgow's Tron Theatre.

I gradually developed confidence and began to enjoy myself, and all of my travels introduced me to hundreds of ordinary Americans I would never have met had I stayed in the showbiz confines of L.A. and New York.

The clubs quickly became too small to accommodate everyone, and I am too darn old to perform three concerts a night anymore, so I began playing larger theatres and achieved a level that I had tried and failed to achieve during my Bing Hitler days.

I also believe that going around the country cemented in my mind the idea that I needed to become a citizen.

It's not that I hadn't thought of it before. My son has been an American-shit since he was born here; I'm an American as well; I simply never worried about the paperwork. But as more people asked me if I was a citizen, I became embarrassed to tell them I wasn't.

Because I'd had a green card for more than five years, I was eligible for consideration, so I applied for naturalisation, and while I waited for the paperwork to be completed, I had some fun with it on the program.

I had remarked on the radio that I had first tasted catfish in the small town of Ozark, Arkansas, and that the mayor of the town had proclaimed me an honorary citizen of Ozark in gratitude for a national TV plug. I reasoned that if I could be named an honorary citizen of Ozark, perhaps other communities might follow suit, putting pressure on the government to consider my application positively.

I mentioned it on the show, and it appeared to hit a chord. The response to my plea was enormous, so much so that we began keeping score, much like an election campaign. We had a giant map with pins where I had been approved, and we made fun of any city that refused to participate. (There was only one--that's right, whatever your name is, mayor of Portland, Oregon. I'm calling you out, you arrogant jerk!)

The show's offices were inundated with proclamations and letters greeting me as an honorary citizen of literally thousands of places across the United States of America.

The tone of the letters was lighthearted--I was made Admiral of the Nebraska Navy, for God's sake--and while everyone seemed to be in on the joke, I got the strong impression from the sack loads of mail that arrived on my desk that Americans understood and appreciated the emotion involved and the decision process I went through on my way to becoming a citizen. What began as a joke on the show evolved into a means for me to convey my appreciation for the welcoming character of the American people. At the close of the Bush-Cheney presidency, everyone was hoping for some nonpartisan and optimistic patriotism.

It seemed to me that politicians had hijacked American patriotism for their own jingoistic objectives, and I wanted to use my television show to move away from that. I wanted to relive the image of the gum-chewing GIs who brought swing dance, fruit, and hope to Scotland when my parents were children. I wanted to express how I felt when I received my large colour poster from NASA in the mail. I wanted as many native-born Americans as possible to experience the excitement and adrenaline of entering the land of the free.

I don't give a rat's a$$ if this sounds trite. I have faith in it. America is without a doubt the best idea for a country that anyone has ever come up with. Not only because we cherish democracy and individual rights, but also because we are always our own most effective dissenting voice. The French may adore Barack Obama, but they did not elect him. We did.

We must never mistake disagreement among Americans on political or moral matters for evidence of patriotism. If you don't agree with what I say or where I stand on some issues, that's fine. I'm grateful we live in America and don't have to oppress one another over it.

We are more than a country. We do not belong to any ethnic group. We are the fulfilment of a long-held desire for justice.

In January 2008, I gladly took the Oath of Allegiance and obtained my citizenship at the Pomona Fairgrounds in Los Angeles, along with three thousand other new Americans from Mexico and none from Scotland.

I took a week off from The Late Late Show to see my mother in Scotland soon before Christmas 2008. mother had been in declining health for a long time; it seemed to me that mother had never truly recovered from her fight with cancer more than a decade before, and she had never been the same since my father died. How could she possibly be? They'd been married for almost fifty years.

I arrived at Glasgow Airport in cold fog on a Saturday night and drove directly to my mother's bedside, undoubtedly imprudent after such a long trip and so little sleep. The roads were slippery, and I wasn't used to driving on the left side of the road.

I was stunned when I finally saw her. Even as I flew over, her condition had deteriorated; she was barely conscious, and I could hear the dreadful sound of pneumonia rattling her bronchi as she struggled to get comfortable.

She'd been in an assisted-living facility for the past two years, and while the staff had been nice and attentive, it was evident to everyone that this was, at long last, the endgame.

I talked to my sleeping mother that night, all day Sunday, and all early Monday, despite being very jet-lagged. I kissed her on the cheek and told her I loved her. I then left her to nap, believing I'd see her later, but she died before I returned. The official cause of death was pneumonia and a kidney ailment, but I believe she died because she couldn't live without my father.

My siblings and I planned her burial for a few days later, and while I waited, I put myself into finishing this book, believing that the job would shield me from the pain, but the words wouldn't come.

So I took a walk.

It was an unusually clear, bright, and frosty day for December in Scotland. Everything appeared sparkling and vividly in focus, but it could simply be my grief. I traversed the streets of Glasgow's West End, where I had roistered and caroused and shattered a few hearts, including my own, so many years ago. I walked into Kelvingrove Park, where the murderous ducks seemed to have been replaced with a much kinder type. I strolled by the gorgeous architecture, the sandstone of the Victorian buildings glistening in the sunlight. I walked and walked and didn't feel anything, but I remembered that from my father's death. Nothing at first, then a never-ending buildup of emotion that threatens to overwhelm you like a winter flood.

I couldn't believe how lovely everything was everywhere I looked. People were flushed from the cold, their breath billowing small clouds of life into the air. The trees were covered with ice crystals, and the clear sky was punctuated by the high vapour trails of distant jetliners.

On Great Western Road, I came to a halt and gazed through the window of a closed art gallery at a Peter Howson painting of a yelling guy and a barking dog. A short chipper gentleman of advanced years, of whom Glasgow has a few, approached and stood next to me.

"Isn't it Craig?" he asked, his accent as thick as soup.

"It is," I said.

He said he recalled me from when I was raising trouble in the church. We didn't know each other; he just saw me around.

"Yer American, noo?" he inquired.

"I am," I said.

"It has to be nice. Nonetheless, you appear Scottish to me. "No offence."

"None taken," I declared.

As I watched him go toward a neighbouring pub, his enormous old-guy ears pink and glistening from the cold, I felt a surge of sympathy for him.

The first broadside of horrible anguish hit me unexpectedly, bursting up and wringing tears from my eyes. I scratched my nose and walked in the opposite direction, pretending my eyes were watering from the cold, which was totally conceivable.

I understood that in my ambition to be an American, I risked forgetting my roots, which would be a heinous act of self-robbery. I realised that I would always adore this spot and that I would bring it with me wherever I went.

I am the offspring of two countries and two parents. My mother gave me blue eyes, and my father gave me tenacity. Scotland shaped me into who I am, and America allowed me to be that person.

America provided me with all I have today. It provided me with a second opportunity at life. A life I had previously mismanaged so disastrously. Americans taught me that failure was only a stage on the path to achievement, not just in terms of profession or riches, but also as a person. I learnt that failure is only failure, and that it can be turned into a story that would make people laugh, and maybe once in a while send a message of hope to others who may be in need.

Becoming an American was not a geographical or even a political decision for me. It was a philosophical and emotional one, founded on a belief in logic and equal opportunity.

I swore an oath not to be intimidated by the might of monarchs and churches. I will not allow any of my children to grow up watching casual animosity between children simply because it has always been that way.

When I became an American, I didn't lose my Scottishness. The two are not incompatible. I am proud of my ancestors. My heart will always be Scottish, but my soul is American, which means that when the choice is between safety and adventure, I choose adventure.

Scottish by birth, American by choice.

Printed in Dunstable, United Kingdom